A Country Boy's Dream Comes True

A Country Boy's Dream Comes True

✦

Travelling the World

Edward Franklin Burkett

iUniverse, Inc.
New York Lincoln Shanghai

A Country Boy's Dream Comes True
Travelling the World

iUniverse, Inc.

For information address:
iUniverse, Inc.
2021 Pine Lake Road, Suite 100
Lincoln, NE 68512
www.iuniverse.com

ISBN: 0-595-32986-1 (pbk)
ISBN: 0-595-66723-6 (cloth)

Printed in the United States of America

Contents

Contents

AUTHOR   FRANK BURKETT
TITLE   PEACE CORPS
TRUE LIFE   ADVENTURE

LIFE

Life is like the wind of a hurricane when you see dark visions in your life and you see no hope of the sun ever shining again. No vision of future whatsoever as if you're a boat on the Ocean and life is a storm rocking you from side to side.

When you try so hard to be the same to one as to the other. When your only desire is to be friend one who hasn't a friend. To be an example of showing some-one love and not just by speaking it. Making them feel loved, wanted and accepted just the way they are.

Even to the strongest one can be so weak if beaten down. we all need love and encouragement for people to make us feel as a kitten while purring if we become the bridge of support to help others out in times of burden.

The greatest joy is not from money but from investing in other people's lives. To be able to share. with them. In such a selfish and cruel world where everyone says to do your own things and the hell with the rest only to blow their minds when someone who comes along who only cares for their well-being.

To have been beaten and made fun of your early years to grow with so much hate that your heart is full of a venom of revenge as if a puppy who never forgets who and what was done him. To treat others who are weaker than you the way the stronger has done you.

In this time you fight back or build a wall around yourself so as not to let hurt and pain in but also to keep love out.

To withdraw into a shell is like taking a flower and covering it up so that the real beauty from within can't be shown or taking the moon-lite voice of the Bob-white and not letting it sing with as much splendor and self confidence that it puts into its singing.

To break the venom of revenge and withdraw one has to be as a vessel that can't hold water but must find a way, a purpose to keep fighting and to live. To see a new world not made up of hurt and pain but joy and peace from within. One has to seek the peace from above for that is the only way hate can be turned into love. Withdrawal into self-confidence. Darkness into light. Dreariness into joy. Only the prince of peace has this to give, so take it.

THE DOG PEN

Growing up in South Alabama from an early age you soon learn that your hunting dog is the most important thing in your life. Talk about my family, pick-em-up truck but don't say anything about my hunting dog. My brother who older than me was no different.

The first dog he got was an awesome sight. His eyes were blood shot red, long ears, drooping mouth and a bark like if you were yelling in a drum full of water. He was a blue tick hound so my brother just called him Blue. Blue was to be a deer dog, but was bred for coon hunting because of his cold nose. I felt of his nose and it was cold. I guess he had a cold but a cold nose meant that he could track a trail several hours old but I didn't know that. Anyway, Ol' Blue was a deer dog if he knew it or not and deer dogs run deer so that the hunter could take what you call a stand on a dirt road and shoot the deer when he crossed. That was the goal. Anyway, Ol' Blue had to have a place to live and my brother started building small houses not only for Ol' Blue but for the 15-30 that was to come later. My brother could build anything but when it came to me, well, let's just say I built one but was scared to let Ol' Blue sleep in it for safety reasons. The dog pen was to me, a 12 year old boy, the learning field of knowledge about the facts of life and the many wonders I was to learn because my brother worked away and taking care of Ol' Blue and the rest was a mans job and I was that man.

Blue's check up—We might not go to the doctor unless we were really sick but Ol' Blue got the best medical treatment you could find any place. One of the first things you learn is if you keep a dog in a pen that he has to go to the bathroom. Then what do you do? You grab a shovel and scoop the dump up and throw it over the fence so you won't step in it and the smell isn't so bad. Next comes worm treatments. You know something is wrong when Ol' Blue takes a dump and you see all these little worms crawling out of his back-end. My brother goes to the Vet and brings these pills with different sizes and colors, sort of like Easter candy and is told to have the dog swallow them but ain't no dog going to do that with his own free will so then what do we do. My brother is a smart guy. He has me to get on Blue's back, open his mouth and throw that beautiful pill in. I then grab Blue's neck and up and down my hand goes until he swallows. I must say I never had a pill break or a dog refuse treatment.

One day you happen to notice Ol' Blue scratching but why? He has fleas and ticks so my brother being he oldest and smartest finds his 50 gallon drum. He fills it full of water and Crisco. The drum is up to my chest but my brother in all his wisdom comes up with the idea of putting the dogs in the drum but how does he get the dogs in the drum without getting wet and dirty. That is where I come in. he says, "Boy, I'm going to show you how easy this is to do, by the time I get back from the store you should be finished." He left and I start A 50 pound dog can't put up much of a fight against a 130 pound 12 year old man but I was wrong. I pick the dog up and it has to be over my head. I then have to put him into the drum but his legs stand straight out and I have to put one leg in at a time until all four legs are in. He doesn't like it too much and is fighting me every step of the way. I then grab his nose and push down on his head, down he goes.

In sort of reminded me of being a pastor giving someone a baptism in the creek but this person didn't want a baptism at all. I then pull him out and he is wet all over and starts shaking water off all over me. He's barking and I'm soaked. It takes me several hours but my job is a success plus I never had to worry about fleas or ticks on me. For some reason they never took to me.

Feeding time—I had watched house dogs eat. If they didn't like it they would turn their noses up to it or just eat a little but not a hound dog. They eat with all the power they had in their body, just like it wasn't ever going to be any other meal coming. My brother had given me orders to feed each dog only half a coffee can full of dry feed because if you didn't they would eat all of his paycheck up along with getting real sick. I did what he said but if my mother comes with me while I was feeding she would say "Oh, they're still hungry, feed them more." Those dogs would eat until their stomachs was as big as a pot-bellied sheriff who would say pass me another piece of that apple pie. Those dogs would eat up two weeks of food in three days. Gosh, was my brother hot not only because of so much food or that they got sick but because of the triple amounts of dog piles we had to shovel out. That was never any fund.

A lot of times if we killed a deer I Would cut the meat up and give it to the dogs. When I threw it to them it never hit the ground. They caught it in mid-air and just inhaled it like a disappearing act in a magic show. One night when I had finished I was rubbing my hands together when Charlie took extreme notice in me. He was a big dog about 70 pounds. He leaped at my hand in mid-air and caught my hand with a full set of beautiful white dog teeth. Down I went to my knees saving uncle or anything else I could think of because he had me and there wasn't a thing I could do about it but call for help. My brother and the Cavalry arrived just in time to save me from Charlie's vice grip on my hand. Oh, what a relief it was for me and a great disappointment for Charlie. It wasn't supper!

Mac's hangover—Mac was our second dog. He was a black and tan short eared dog. He had a bark that was like Hank Williams' yodel. He along with his sister, Molly, was the best darn deer dogs ever seen in Alabama or the world. None were better than them. It was on a Friday afternoon. The day before my brother was to be home early that Saturday morning to go hunting that I did a bad thing. My brother always keeps a cooler of beer at the dog pen. I never drank any myself but it was always there for anybody that wanted it. The devil was in me so I took a can and opened it, poured it out in Mac's bowl but he wouldn't drink it so I mixed it with a little food and down it went. Well, Mac didn't look drunk so I did the same with two more cans. By that time he was running around in circled yelling. I had never seen a dog act so crazy before. The other dogs didn't know what to do with him either. After about an hour I left to go to the house. I went to bed that night and was awakened about 4:00 in the morning by my brother getting me up to go hunting. I had forget that I had given a 50 pound dog three cans of beer the afternoon before. Me and my brother put all the dogs in a dog box on the back of the truck. I had noticed I didn't hear Mac's voice so I went to pull him out of the house. He wouldn't come! I pulled harder and he belched in my face and I smelt the beer. I knew then, Mac had a hang-over and my brother was going to be mad at me not only for getting Mac drunk but wasting his good beer like that. I picked up Mac's body as fast as I could and put him in the dog box. Away we drive until we found deer tracks on the dirt road and let the dogs out. Mac came out slow with my encouragement. My brother noticed something then and there. He said "What is wrong with Ol' Mac?" I said very fast, "Nothing", all the time keeping him away from Mac in case he belched again. Mac wouldn't do a thing all day long, just grunt and groan. A few days later I heard two hunters talking. One had found Ol' Mac on the road after the hunt and picked him up to put him in the dog box and Mac belched. The hunter then asked me was my brother using a new kind of dog feed. I said, "No sir." The hunters then said that was the strangest thing he had ever seen in all the years of hunting and I asked what. He said "I swear I believe Ol' Mac was drunk and had a hang-over but then who in the world would give beer to a dog. I said "No one would do something that stupid" and he agreed and walked away.

Football—When fall of the year came along, we knew another big event was in the making. Football season! This was the 1970's before cable or the T.V. dish but good old fashioned radio. 1:30 every Saturday 5 to 10 trucks would start rolling down the hill towards the dog pen. All men, no woman to listen to the Alabama Crimson Tide play football. Who were these men? Some had a high school degree, no one had been to any University much less the University of Alabama but they never missed a Saturday. It was like going to church. It was an uplifting experience. Why then were we wanting Alabama to win? Well we were Southern men. We were the only American males to lose a war, the Civil War. Alabama was known for Hank Williams, Stand in the schoolhouse Door and the Selma to Montgomery March but we wee also known for something else. Not many people are known on a first name basis, Elvis, The Beatles, Wallace and The Bear. Paul Bryant, head coach of the University of Alabama just like General Lee in charge of the Southern Army. Coach Bear Bryant would take our state name Saturday after Saturday into victory over some Northern school. The guys at the dog pan would role on the dirt if Alabama scored or give out the loudest rebel yell you had ever heard. All the dogs would be barking over all the excitement. None of us had ever met the Bear but we all believed after the win that we would have been welcome at his home for supper. He brought us so much pride. Coach Bryant was just a good Ol' boy who made good.

Birds and Bee—My brother always had s rather large supply of girlie books that he kept at the dig pen. So with my 12 year old mind and a few cousins we would sneak down there and look as if we were really doing something bad or sinful because of our curiosity over the female anatomy. They sure had some beautiful bodies and the big picture in the center was the best of all. It sort of made your tongue hand out like a dog. The reason I know that was, Ol' Molly was in heat. That means that she is ready for a boyfriend so we took Ol' Blue out of the pen and no one told Blue what to do. He looked as if he learned that a long time ago. He mounted her, his tongue hanging out. We understood that part O.K. but it wasn't long before they were butt to butt still connected. We just couldn't understand that part too well. When they got unhooked we put them back in their different pens. A few months later, Molly started to get big. My brother was upset because he didn't want her to have puppies this time of year. He said keep an eye on her every morning to see if she starts having puppies so every morning before school I would go down to the dog pen and check. One morning I checked and she had two. I went running back to the house to get Mama. She had more experience at babies than I did. When we arrived back at the dog pen tow more had been born. Mama said just let her alone. Molly knows what to do. That afternoon when I got home from school, I went to the dog pen to check on Molly. She was doing O.K. but this time I counted 10 puppies. My brother said to me, "Pick the puppy you want" I was so happy, my first hunting dog so far some strange reason I chose a female and a runt at that. I named her Kate.

Little Kate—Little Kate was such a loving dog. She would lick me all over the face, run up and down hills but Kate was a hunting dog, not a play dog so when deer season opened I just knew she had to be good. She had to be, she was my deer dog. Good, you better believe it! Everybody bragged on Kate. I felt 10 feet tall. I was so proud of my Little Kate. Towards the end of the season a big man by the name of Ray told everybody that his big Ol' black and tan Toby could find a deer faster and out run Kate any old day. Ray had loved Toby so much that he even hired an artist to paint a giant size picture of Toby to hang in his living room. I took Big Ray's challenge. The day and time was set. It was a cold day. My brother and junior turned both Little Kate and Toby out. We all listened. I think all the hunters were pulling for me because I had never won at anything and I was only 12 years old. As the hours passed we heard them coming but not together. I was worried Kate was on the wrong trail and then shots were fired. We all got in the truck to see who shot. Sure enough someone had shot and a deer lay dead. Now it was a wait and see game to see which dog came out of the woods first, Toby or Kate and then all of a sudden out of the woods came a dog. Was it Little Kate or Toby? We couldn't tell, so Big Ray in a mule's voice said TOBY but no answer. I then yelled KATE and here she came as fast as she could. Everybody patted me on the back. It felt so good, me and Kate had won. Someone asked Big Ray what happened. He said Toby's hair was too long and he got too hot. A few weeks later I went down to feed the dogs after a big rain. I found Kate. She had been on a chain and jumped over the fence but the chain was too short. She was cold and dead. I unhooked her and dug a hole to bury her. I cried when I put the dirt over her body because I had lost not only a dog but the best friend I ever had.

Frank Burkett

This story only was published 8years ago

MARIO

I was a Peace Corps volunteer in Micronesia, State of Pohnpei where I was an English teacher in 1986-87. My students were so poor that most didn't have shoes, one pair of pants and two shirts for a year. One for Sunday church and one for school. 12 English books for 75 students. We had a pen pal project between my students on Pohnpei and American students. The American students were always talking about material things and my students talked about the beautiful flowers, waterfalls and colorful birds. My go between in American asked didn't my students feel bad because they didn't have what the American kids had. My reply was "Pohnpeian students don't know anything about a swimming pool but they have the Pacific Ocean. They think it's more important to talk to each other than listen to a stereo but then they have never heard a stereo. To them food and family were the most important things. You were a rich person not on what you owned but on what you gave away in your time and money so my reply was "If you never had it, you never missed it."

Mario was one of my students. He was mixture of Spanish and Polynesian. His body was small but firm from eating only rice all his life. His eyes were of so much kindness and he was so gentle, polite with every one. He was so cute and lovable that you just wanted to give him a big hug. He was 14 but he looked much younger with a beautiful smile surrounded by his smooth copper colored skin.

It was Christmastime and my students had given me 10 present. Some of the presents were a pencil, bar of soap, comb and even a nicely wrapped cucumber. It was the best Christmas I had ever had because my students had given me the best they had.

I invented Mario and three other boys to go into town with me on Christmas Eve. We had to walk one hour because there are few cars and every place you go you walk or don't go. Anyway we arrived at one of the three restaurant in Kolonia. The boys had never been to a restaurant much less sitting at a table in a soft chair. I ordered everybody a coke float. These boys were so happy because it tasted so good. They had never had a Coke or Ice Cream before, so it was a treat.

Time and time again Mario would climb a coconut tree and bring me a coconut or pineapple. You see in his culture when you do something good for somebody then that person has to do something good for you because it's a small island and everybody has to get along because you have no place else to go.

One day Mario was late in getting to class but when he did I noticed he couldn't walk so I went up to him. The sight made me sick! One of his eyes was closed shut, his face was puffed up twice its size. I took him to my place where I had first-aid kit. He took off his shirt and had bruise spots all over his chest and back.

I said "Who did this to you, Mario." "Why?" he just looked at me and smiled the best that he could. I said "How can you smile, Mario, because I am as mad as I can be at the people who did this to you." You see Mario was a Christian and he took the part about Jesus turning the other check at just that.

He went on to tell me how four older boys had jumped him and the sickening things they did to his body. I said, "Mario, you are so kind to everybody how could anybody have hated you this much. He said they didn't. I was walking on the road and I heard these buys saying bad things about my friend. I told them to stop. I said that he was a good man, he would put his arm around me, buy me coke and ice cream, he was so very king to me and my classmates and then they jumped me. I said "Mario, who could this person be that you took a beating for and why." He looked up at me with one eye closed and said "You, and why because you were good to me." I was floored! I cried together with Mario with our arms around each other. I had never had anybody take a beating for me before, especially one so young and so small just because he loved me so much for being kind to him.

Frank Burkett

1

FLYING OFF TO THE WILD BLUE YONDER

When I got accepted into the Peace Corps, they asked me if I wanted to go to a place called Micronesia and I first thought they said micro-Asia, but I soon found out. About the only thing I knew about Micronesia was that it was between Australia and the philippines, much else I was pretty much lost on. Well, I loaded up in my home here in Butler County and went off to Montgomery, Alabama to catch the airplane. It was the first time I'd ever flown on an airplane, so I got on the airplane with fourteen people, it was a twin-engine. I have to say I was very scared. I'd never been shaken so much or shook so much in my whole life as getting on that little airplane and taking off. I didn't know if I'd ever land again. Well, luckly enough I did, I went on into Atlanta, Georgia—a humongous sized airport and while I was there I changed planes, got on a plane going to Los Angeles, California. Well, when I got to Los Angeles, I was lost. I had never been an airport, much less flown on an airplane, much less know where to find my luggage. I was lost! While there at the airport, I didn't realize it but on the same plane that flew in with me was the television actor Claude Akins, TV star from Sheriff Lobo, Movin' On, Larado. I said, "Oh, gosh, I've actually met a movie star." There he is. I said, "Well, I want to go talk to him." I went up to him and he was the nicest man that you'd ever want to meet. He helped me find my luggage, showed me what line to get into, told me about his acting career, what he'd be going in the future. He was so nice, so friendly, so helpful. His wife was there. She didn't say much. Pretty soon his chauffeur drove up in a limosine and I watched as his chauffeur put his bags in the car and drove off. That was quite an experience for me to meet a movie star like that. Then we loaded up in Los Angeles and headed off to Hawaii, we were on a 747. I get on that plane and it's twenty-three seats across. It looks four times the size of a football field to me. I said, "Goodness gracious! How un the world is this plane going to take off?"

While we're taking off, it does alright, no trouble, it gets on the runway and the thing just jams up the engines—whmmmm, whmmmm, whmmwhmm, whmm, whmm, racing the engines. While the engines are racing, I'm scared. Anyway, we fly over the Pacific Ocean from Los Angeles to Hawaii. While in Hawaii, we get there, I guess, at ten o'clock at night, get a taxi, that's the first time I ever road in a taxi cab. Pretty unusual. I was wondering what he would charge me. I looked up there and the further we drove to the hotel the Peace Crops had for us, the more I was seeing that it would cost money to get on that thing. I was worried about how much money it would be. Turned out to be about $10.00, which I guess was pretty good. While I was in Hawaii, I said to myself, "Well, I've met Mr. Claude Akins." I was looking around, "Well, maybe I'll meet Tom Selleck or jack Lord." Neither one of them worked, didn't meet any more movie stars.

ON THE AIRPLANE

The seats were real small, for my big frame, which is six-three, two hundred forty-five pounds. But, they're pretty comfortable after you get to sitting in them for twelve hours. Your butt goes numb! I was wondering, on the airplane, while I was sitting there, "Where in the world are the toilets?" and being a Southerner, I wouldn't ask something like that, so I said, "I'll just follow the line." and I did, sure enough, they went exactly where it was. It's still amazing to me how you can be flying so high and so fast and get up and walk around on that thing. They show movies on there, a little screen that's so small you've got to squint your eyes to look at it, but you put earphones on and at least you can hear it. On the airplane they're always feeding you, every time you turn around they're wanting to give you something to drink. Never could get no rest. I guess we must have flown thirty hours—that's after we left Hawaii. Times change, I didn't know what time it was, daylight, nighttime seemed like it was going every which-a-way. The more we traveled it seemed the stranger the time got and the daylight got. I guess that's what they call jet lag, where when you leave one area you gain a day and you come back the next time you lose a day. I think that's the way it works. Anyway I was pretty tired. I guess that's what all the Presidents call jet lag.

ARRIVAL IN MICRONESIA
STATE OF POHNPEI

Well, upon our arrival at Pohnpei Airport, I hadn't been too used to many airports anyway. All of a sudden I got off the plane and felt the humidity coming off into my face. Oh, it was so hot coming off that plane after being in that air-conditioning. As you walk down towards where you pick up your baggage you look at all these kids at the fence and I mean it's just covered in kids! All these little brown-skinned, black-eyed people, didn't wear no shirts, wearing flip-flops, staring at me. I felt like I was an animal in a zoo! Pretty soon I realized I was quite different from the local population. At the airport, they bring you up in a bus, they look through your luggage, all of a sudden, they loaded our bags on a truck. They were driving on a paved road, passing on a hill, one Peace Corps girl looked up in the front and said, "No one is driving." I looked, sure enough there wasn't, on the driver's side there was no steering wheel, the steering wheel was on the right-hand side. I said, "Wow!" We arrived at the hotel Pohnpei, that's where we were going to say. The drivers took our bags off and left. They assigned rooms with apartments. I looked at the rooms and the first thing I noticed was they were thatched. They had a small front porch, small cots, they had a fan—we had electricity. The shower was a beautiful place inside your little room. It was rocks, beautiful flowers all over the place, looked like the <u>Garden</u> <u>of</u> <u>Eden.</u> But the water was on only from about five o'clock to eight o'clock. That was strange to me because I found out Pohnpei has the most rainfall of any place in the world, and for them to ration your water? At night the owners would give you a mosquito coil, that was to keep the mosquitoes away. Some of the rooms had a small icebox but mine didn't.

FIRST MEETING

As soon as we got there the Peace Corps staff wanted to get us together to have a meeting. We walked into the meeting place and there was a large container full of water. I got some of it. I couldn't believe it but the water was hot. I said "Oh gosh, What have I gotten myself into?" I found out the Peace Corps staff had boiled the water and didn't have refrigeration to cool it. I looked on the wall and it had a news release from some place in the world, Israel had bombed somebody in Lebanon. Right then I realized there was no TV or daily paper and any kind of news is good. They had a mailbox here for our outgoing mail. Strangely enough with me after the first day I was there, I was looking to get mail from home. Strange, for I realized it would take seven to fourteen days to get there. One of the rules they gave us when we got there is anytime you walk into a place, you take your shoes off. Well, that's okay unless you've got work boots on, that gets pretty hard trying to get work boots off. They told the women to wear long skirts, down to their knees or below, travel in groups and don't drink water that is not boiled. The water thing, after spending many years hauling hay, I realized that I needed a lot of water and a lot of salt so I found me a place where I could buy distilled water at $1.00 a gallon, you could get it for a dollar a gallon if you didn't have it cooled. If you wanted it cool, you had to pay $1.85 a gallon. I found out that I'd do that during my whole stay on Pohnpei, buy distilled water.

NIGHTLIFE

The nightlife while we were there during our pre-service training reminded me of sitting on the front porch at the house, like on Andy Griffin, the way Andy and Barney used to sit on the porch on the Andy Griffin Show. That's what we did, most of the time—just shooting the breeze. We'd go out to eat, there were about six different places to eat. It wasn't the best in the world to eat, it was a small place mostly fish, they had chicken. We were so scared to drink the water because they had told us that we might get hepatitis or something so we usually bought a soft drink. It gets pretty old after a while if you drink soft drinks all day long, when I couldn't get to my water place for $1.85. You come into the nightlife and they've told you so much about being culturally sensitive that you're scared to walk or hiccup much less talk because you don't want to be insensitive. You want to fit into the culture. One of the Peace Corp girls was at her porch and this fifteen year old boy came up to her and he had a towel on and he took the towel and opened it up and what he told her in doing that was, we found out later, that he was a man. That was quite an interesting thing that came up, while we were staying at the Hotel Pohnpei. The Peace Corps girl's father was a Southern Baptist preacher and she had never even seen a stick person much less a naked boy. Her face turned three shades of red! All of a sudden all of the young ladies in the group were asking me to walk with them. I said, "Well, I might be popular, but it's beginning to be noticeable to me that all these young ladies are wanting me to walk around with them." I found out that the reason for this is because on Pohnpei, according to their culture, if you're considered married, that way, if you're considered married, then the young man leave you alone. So with all the young women walking around me, I had a reputation very early for having many, many wives. We were walking one night and this young guy came up to us and said, "Oh, it's good to see Ronald Reagan is doing a good job." I asked "What do you mean?" "He has sent you over here to teach us English." We walked by the pool hall one night and found that the people from the outer islands were not accepted in the pool hall, and knew they'd better not go into the pool hall. They told us that the people from the outer islands couldn't go into the pool halls. The same way blacks were treated in the South. This same guy said "We'll trade you Pohnpeian women for American women." Didn't go along with that trade too good.

FIRST CAMP-OUT

The Peace Corps was entertaining us and making us feel welcome after we landed on Pohnpei. We were still at the Hotel Pohnpei. They wanted us to get together and come up with several recreational programs. One of these thing was camp-outs. As you know, when you get a group of people together everybody wants to be <u>chief</u>, with not many Indians to do the work. This was no different. There were forty-eight of us and I sat back and listened because I had planned camp-outs for years and years and wasn't too thrilled going on camp-outs anymore, especially when it was going to be on a small island. I didn't like going over the water to get there. Some of them planned our menus and we loaded the boat and went out to it. When we got to the island all of a sudden the ones who planned the menus realized that we had no electric stove, no microwave, no running water. We've got all this food and forty-eight people, and we're on an island with no electricity. "What're we going to do?" and they started looking at each other. I took over, started a fire, got two grill tops they found on the beach, make-shift. A Southern girl from Louisiana helped me cook the chicken and rice and I cooked the chicken over an open fire. Those forty-eight people were so hungry that I couldn't get the chicken done before they wanted to eat it. I had a bottle of tabasco sauce. I said, "I want some of this chicken, you mess with my chicken, I'll fight you." I started sprinkling tabasco sauce on top of the chicken to, maybe, slow them down a little bit. Would you believe it didn't slow them down one bit! They ate that chicken with the tabasco sauce on the top of it. Didn't make any difference. I got a few pieces of chicken. On the island you could go out into the ocean, walk out there, see all kinds of fish, stingray, sharks, the water was so blue, coconut trees, banana trees everywhere, sandy beaches. I guess they say it was made in Heaven but I just wasn't too impressed with all that sand, and especially all that water. I guess I was looking for pine tree and grass.

MEDICAL PREP TALK

For about a week every day the Peace Corps nurse would tell us how to take care of our medical needs in a Third-World Nation.

I never knew you could talk so much about going to the bathroom as much as we did. We were taught how to get a stool specimen from an out-house and that's not easy if you've ever been in one, it's about six feet past the little sitting hole and you're just not going to put your arm down inside the hole. Plus all these worms crawling around at the bottom.

We were told that the average person on Pohnpei lived to the age of 57. Tuberculosis was wide spread over the island but the thing that really got my attention was leprosy. The only place I had ever heard of leprosy was in the Bible and how bad those people had been treated. I was concerned about that but the nurse said we didn't have anything to worry about but that it could show up in us 30 years down the road. She said that there was medicines which could cure it now. That really opened our eyes.

MEDICAL KIT—HEALTH CARE

Everybody was given a medical kit. The Peace Corps who were on the outer islands were given anti-biotic drugs. We were told that they were for us only and nobody else but when I got to my village, I found out that I was soon to get the title of "Dr. Burkett" because I did a lot of first-aid on mostly children. I couldn't sit back and watch anybody suffer when I had the means and knowledge to help. If it was too bad, I would walk with them to the hospital which was about a forty minute walk for me.

The hospital was run by locals but the doctors were mostly from the United Nations. A few Americans who might be working off a student loan. Most of the doctors were from India, Pakistan, or some other nation. Anyway there was never more than 5 doctors at any given time. The United Nations furnished the drugs and several times would run out. Because of the shortages of doctors, the government gave E.M.T.'s the same responsibility as a doctor would have. Five doctors for over 21,000 people.

DEPARTURE

After all that training we were ready to start so the Peace Corps who were going to Yap, Truk and Kosar left in the early morning hours, leaving only the ones who were staying on Pohnpei.

We knew that we would be living with a training family at some place called Palikar but that's about all we knew. They told us that they had held training for our host-families so that they would understand what to look for when these strange Americans arrived to live in their homes.

We're in a different world, customs, language and we are going to move into a person's home. How do we act, what do we say, what will we eat, what, what, what if? We were all looking forward to it but it's just something about not knowing.

Peace Corps had told the families about each of us and they choose us by that. I asked who got me as if it would help and they said a man, wife and two kids who wanted the biggest and the strongest. I said they must want someone to dig ditches, or carry an awful big load of something. "Oh Lord, what have I got into!"

2

MOVING IN WITH A FAMILY

When we left the Hotel Pohnpei after about fourteen days of being together, all the other volunteers went to different places. The ones on Pohnpei stayed there. We went up a long road and the roads, after the few paved roads that were in town Kolonia, I noticed they were white. I looked down closer and saw that their dirt roads were scattered with coral reef like we would use gravel or slag on a road that we didn't put an asphalt top on. We went to a school called Palikar for training. I was the last one picked up for moving in with a family. Then I met him, my host father. He said, "I wanted the biggest and the strongest so that's what I got." He was a nice enough looking gentleman, real friendly, real outspoken. So I loaded up in the truck with him. It was a beat-up truck that shook and rattled, we road down a road with holes as big as the truck itself, went about three miles. Finally we stopped. A bunch of young boys grabbed my luggage and went off down through the middle of the jungle, I followed him, luckily I had my work boots on. I got covered in mud. He didn't get any mud on him, the family didn't either. We walked for about twenty minutes to a cute little house in the middle of nowhere. I have to say that he lived so far back in the woods that to me you'd have to ride a pregnant donkey in there to be able to get out. The second night my family, my host father's family, had a sickness in the family. So I was left in the middle of nowhere with two boys, ages eleven and nine and neither one could speak much English. I'm stuck in the middle of nowhere with no electricity, kerosene lamp, didn't know how to get out if I needed to, there was no telephone, in the middle of the swamp. That was pretty scary for the first three nights.

TRAGEDY HAPPENS

Our third day we were there one of our Peace Corps girls, a trainee, was raped. She was walking on her way from school to her host family, it was pouring rain, and this guy showed up out of nowhere. It just happened to be that that day she was by herself. It was her third day there. He put a machete up to her and told her that if she fought back, he would kill her. She didn't and up until this day, I don't believe the guy was ever captured. It wasn't long after that that the family put, I guess you would call them bodyguards, with us. We had a meeting, and they were talking about keeping kids around us all the time. I asked "What good is a kid gonna do if somebody wants to hurt you?" What it was we later found out was if someone is around in that family, no one will bother you because they'll lose face. My host grandfather at that time decided that it was best for me to move in up with his family. So I left the swamp to move up beside the road. Anyway, while we were there, during our training, an eighteen year old boy had died.

THE FUNERAL

It was about our third week there, and as I was saying, an eighteen year old youth had died while climbing up the mountain. They said he had a heart attack. Peace Corps said go to the funeral. Anyway, it was a good idea, the Peace Corps thought of it, that they'd send us to the funeral to get more involved in the culture. At the funeral there were a lot of people. It was hot, files everywhere, and we still don't know anything, we're just very innocent little babes there. Well, here they come up the road bringing a big pig. They brought this pig and laid the pig down. A big old pig, an all the people that are in the village are sitting there. They take a machete out and cut the throat of the pig and they leave the pig there, and he's grunting and the blood is just squirting out and all these volunteers are sitting there. That was about to turn everybody a little sick. Then they brought up these little bags. Looked like a corn sack with something in it that was moving. Well, this man took a big stick and whammed down on the bag, and everybody was saying, "Whoa, what's going on here?" So, they went and opened the sacks up, and it was <u>dogs</u>, and that's when we got a good initiation. All the volunteers started filling out one-by-one. While we were there at the funeral we noticed that the family builds the casket, digs the hole and buried it. There's no funeral home on Pohnpei.

DAILY LIFE

Well, the eating first, I guess we'll talk about. I would eat first and whatever food that I left on my plate, the family would come and eat it. That's how it worked, eat on the floor, most of the other family members ate with their fingers but they had forks for me to eat with. The bathing was done in a river and I would go down to the river and take a bath, you'd wear a towel, down a steep hill. A lot of times I'd have to run an eel away. Eels at the bottom of the hill about as long as my arm and about as big as my arm and he didn't like to give up his place of residency. While I was down there at the river, I found giant crawfish, as big as your hand, they liked white toes. Sleeping arrangements were, the family had one mattress and since I was the guest, they'd usually give me that mattress, while everybody else slept on the floor. We would put a mosquito coil down at night so the mosquitoes wouldn't bother us. We had an outhouse. They built it just for us—me and another volunteer living there. We had a key, all the outhouses over there have keys—that's a good outhouse. If you've ever been around a bad outhouse and smelled it, you know a bad outhouse. Anyway, we had a lock on it, that was to keep the little kids out, also we were the honored guest.

STORIES FROM MY GRANDFATHER

My grandfather in my family was one of the nicest men I've ever met in my life. He was as kind and considerate as any person I've ever met anywhere in the world. Easy-going, relaxing, he was not what I guess you'd call a typical Pohnpein man. But the stories he told me. we would talk for hours and hours and hours, were wonderful and will stay with me a lifetime. One of the stories that he told me was about a missionary. I think he was a Protestant missionary, anyway, he was on the island many, many years ago. The people in the village where he lived took him one day and got mad with him because of what he was preaching and put a rock around his neck with a rope and carried him out to the reef and threw him in the water, and he died. Well, they call that the curse and by that these particular people in this village, up until this day, go missing—well, then they don't get particularly worried about it because they feel that they're paying for the sins of their ancestors, who killed a missionary. My grandfather was of Japanese descent. He told me of many cruelties that the Japanese people applied on the people of Pohnpei. He told me a story called The Coconut Tree. World War this Pohnpein man had a coconut tree. This Japanese solder told the man that it was his coconut tree. The man said no it wasn't and he had his soldiers hold the man down and he took his sword I should say and he cut the man's hand off. Then the other hand because he wouldn't tell the Japanese that it was his tree. Well the man died and many years later, to the present time, this same soldier came back to visit Pohnpei as a curse and the people in that village found out that he was coming, an old man now, and they sent word, that if he came to this village that his family would kill him. So the Japanese tourist left. Japanese used forced labor to make all the roads on the island, with bayonets, slave labor. The Japanese had a plan that if the Americans attacked the islands, they would take the Pohnpeins and make them run into the Americans so that they would be used as a buffer zone. We sat for many hours and he told me many stories about his life and I will never forget.

SECOND CAMP-OUT

Peace Corps is still on us about these darn camp-outs and I'm not too fond of them and not too fond of the water either. We were in training one day, we had a camp-out coming up that week-end. One of the teachers asked the Peace Crops staff if we would go out to Ant Atoll if the waves are high. I said, "What do you mean high?" He said anywhere between twenty-five and thirty feet high. So I raised my hand, never having been out in the ocean I didn't understand what he was talking about. Of course the Peace Corps staff said, "Sure, we're going anyway, regardless." Well that weekend came up, a few of us loaded in different boats, with like a Johnson power motor on the back, they gave us life jackets, we go outside, we go through the reefs, once we hit that, we end up in the South Pacific Ocean. The wave are <u>that high in that little boat</u>. I am scared for my life! I say my prayers, glad that I have already wrote my Mother and Father on that Friday, so if I didn't come back…sitting in the boat. I had my lifejacket on, we had a big thermos jug on the boat and I had that between my legs, I held on to the rope, in case we went over I could still hold on. The waves were so high, it was dark, cloudy. I was the most scared I've ever been in my life. Well, when we crossed the ocean and went to the other side this elderly lady with us, her name was Ruth, I met her on the bank. She looked at me, I looked at her and I said, "Ruth, are you thinking the same thing I am?" and she said, "What's that?" I said, "Well, I think you and me have got a miserable weekend coming up." Anyway, that night I didn't realize how cold it would get on the beach and I got freezing cold, on that beach where we had to sleep. I went and took some coconut limbs, cut them off and I got down and put those things on top of me and I slept. None of the other volunteers knew where I was, but I stayed warm. While we were there they told us a little about how important fishing was. The kids as soon as they could walk were carried out into the ocean. They spear fished, or they used lines and hooks, or fish nets while we were there they were going to show us how to use the fishnet and this particularly dangerous fish stuck a lady, while she was trying to pick it up in the net, in the leg. I don't know what kind of fish it was but it was poison. But the guides, our trainers, right away cut the fish open, took the insides out and put them on her leg and she never got sick. It was their Pohnpein medicine and from what I gathered from what other people told me if that hadn't happened, she would have probably got sick and maybe even died. We packed up to head back home. As I said, I knew we had a return trip. I said,

"Lord, if you'll let me get out of here, I'll do something good the rest of my life."
Making all kind of promises. Well, we made it through okay, my boat did. In
fact, we were the first to make it through. But we lost about three other boats,
and it took a few hours before we were able to get them back. The finally came in
and I have to say that was my last time of ever going out on a boat again. I don't
like water period and I'll never go again.

TEACHING SEX EDUCATION

This is a story that was told to us true and I think it is true. They had a Peace
Corps volunteer that had come there many years before and he wanted to teach
the people on the island about birth control. Well, the island has 21,000 people
and 75% under age 15. Some families have up to as many as 22 children. So this
guy went to his host father one day and said "Okay, I'm going to show you how
you don't have to have no more babies no more." The host father said okay. The
reason they have so many children is one thing when the Germans were there
they pretty well killed off close to all the men in this particular village and it was
lucky that three boys escaped, and these three boys, that's how the race of the
Pohnpeins continued. Another reason they have so many children is when the
parents are old, they expect the children to take care of them. That's why they
have so many children. But getting back to training sex education he told his host
father "I'm going to give you something and you use this thing, you won't make
babies." He said "Okay." So he brought out a box of contraceptives and he gave
his host father one and remember this guy didn't know what they were. He'd
never read a newspaper or watched television or anything. The guy said you put
this on and his host father said "Well, where do you put it?" and he said—I
always have s joke that he must have been a Southern Baptist, because they don't
talk about things like this—so the guy reached over in the corner and pulled out
a broomstick and he took the broomstick and put the contraceptive in it—the
broomstick and he said "Now, everynight before you go to bed you put this thing
on and you won't have any more children." Well, the volunteer left and he came
back a few years later and he was talking to his host father again and his host
father reached and pulled out the contraceptives and give them back to him and
he said, "Why are you giving me these?" Didn't you use them?" and he said,
"Awhile I used them, but," he said, "I have three more children," He said,
"Didn't you use them like I said?" he said, "I sure did, I put one on the broomstick every night before I went to bed and pot it in the corner and I still had many
children."

MARLIN PERKINS "WILD KINGDOM"

I had grown up watching Marlin Perkins "Wild Kingdom" so sitting in your home in Alabama you never think you'll see any of these animals that Jim and Marlin catch and tag on TV but one day I got a ride during training on the back of a Toyota pick-up truck. I stepped in and I say the biggest turtle or sea turtle I had ever seen. In fact, the only one I've ever seen. That turtle was dead, caught during the night by a fisherman. I never guessed in a million years that I would see one not on "Wild kingdom" but in person and in the flesh. That turtle covered the back end of the truck. It fed twelve people for several days but I didn't get in on that feast so I never ate any giant turtle soup.

TRACK-FIELD NO RESTROOMS

During training we had the holiday of Liberation Day. A day that the Pohnpeians have to celebrate the American's defeat of Japan. It is during the week you have the games. Track-field, swimming, war canoe races against each other. Sort of like Alabama playing Auburn but it was Nett against VH.

It rained just about all day and I was soaked. I had only been there about two months and this was the first public event I had went to. Well my stomach was hunting something bad, I mean like it had never before hurt. I had to go to the restroom but there wasn't an unless it had a lock on it. And I didn't have a key. I'd sit down, stand up, walk trying to stop the pain and nothing helped. My mama had always told me to wear clean underwear so in case I was to have to go to the hospital, I'd have clean underwear on and here I was a grown man about to use the bathroom in his pants. The place was crowded with people so I took off as fast as I could to the jungle. I had just gotten my pants down and I went. Oh, what a relief it was! Nothing had never felt better!

FRED GETS A HEAD-ACHE

One day during training I was on the back of Fred's truck. Fred was one of our trainers. He taught us the language and some culture. Anyway We were driving along the road and he stopped to pick up some grass along side the road. I asked Fred what was the grass for. He said for a headache. Oh, Fred I have some Tylenol. Fred said no, Pohnpeian medicine was very strong. We were surrounded by a lot of Pohnpeians. Three hours went by and when I was alone, Fred came up and asked me for some Tylenol. I said Pohnpeian medicine didn't help. He said, "Oh, it helped, but it was a bad, bad head-ache."

GRAND OPENING

My family talked about World War as if it was only yesterday. You know like we use to sit on the front porch and talk about the good ole days well they do the same on Pohnpei but there is some different and that is you can still find Japanese tanks along the road or a giant hole made by U.S. planes dropping bombs on the Japanese. Anyway my family told of how they used to come to town on a water ox and you couldn't travel but on road just a little way and then have to turn back because there was no road around the island.

The U.S. Military has a C.A.T. Team base of twelve men. They build roads and repair them. They hire locals to cook for them and about once a month they have a C-130 air drop supplies to them. They give out first aid to the locals and every Friday night they show a big screen movie free to all the Pohnpeians and that is a big event for everybody.

The C.A.T. Team built a road around the island. When it was open anybody and everybody who had any kind of truck, car or bike was asked to join in on the Grand Opening of the new road. I had never heard so many horns in all my life. I would say that there were about 50 trucks in a parade going around the island. You have never seen so many happy people. Everybody had big smiles! It was a beautiful ride. Greenery, flowers of every color and size. Pigs, chickens and dogs running wild. You could only travel about 15 miles an hour and that took several hours to travel one side to the other on the island because the road was made of coral, Sorta like rocks the size of cups.

3

HISTORY, CLIMATE AND A LITTLE CULTURE WITH LOVING

Micronesia is made up of four island states, Pohnpei, Truk, Yap and Coshri. All have a different language, all have a different culture. The Federated States of Micronesia is what they are called. In the Federated States of Micronesia there are 607 islands, 65 are inhabited, they are members of the Caroline Island chain. They are spread oner a million square miles of the Pacific Ocean. They lie 3 degrees below the Equator, the daily temperature and the climate is 80 or the low nineties. The night lows are thirteen degrees cooler, rainfall is six inches could be a day, or a hundred or two hundred inches a year. The humidity stays at 80 percent all the time. Vegetation is very lush, all over the islands beautiful orchids, waterfalls, and the reason is because the humidity is so high, you can plant a watermelon seed and in there days it's up.

ARRIVAL OF OUTSIDERS

Micronesian culture was quite well developed at least 1200 or 1400 AD. In the 1700s they were introduced to four powers who came to have a strong influence over them. They were the Spanish, German, Japanese and the Americans. It is said on the island that the Spanish came for God, the Germans for gold, the Japanese glory, and Americans came to stay. Remember as you read the rest of my book that all these countries ruled the Micronesians and up until they came under the control of the United States, they had no say-so in their own destiny. They're under a compact of free association with the United States. It gives the Micronesians the same citizenship rights that we have. A lot of the students, the young people on the island take advantage of joining our military forces. Twenty percent of the island has electricity, there are a few old trucks there. A little about their culture!

CULTURE, TIDBITS—A MELTING POT IF THE RACES OF MAN—SPANISH, GERMANS, JAPANESE AND THE AMERICANS

Pohnpeins are generally a threw-together society. They have yams, taro, banana, papaya, pineapple, coconut—all that is grown on the island. Cucumbers. Some of the different variations in their culture is like this: If someone hate me and I'm Pohnpein: getting back to the hate part, as I was saying, if you hate me on Pohnpei, no matter how much you hate me, if I did something good for you, then you would have to do the same kind of goodness in return to me. Third party—if you have a problem with someone on the island you don't go to them and talk, a direct confrontation. Pohnpeins are not for confrontations. You go through a third party and you tell them what you feel and pretty soon it gets back to the one that you want it to get to. A group on Pohnpei is far more important than an individual. The family is the group structure. It's more important than the individual. When you're on Pohnpei, the people will tell you what you want to hear, or, what they think you want to hear. One of the things on the island that you'll run into is they never tell you all they know, because if hey do then they'll die. It's part of their custom. The family—the men are honored on the island, especially the older men, the women take second place. Women are to be seen and hot heard. In the family linkage the youngest member in the family gets the least. The biggest celebration in the island is birthdays, but after the first year, what I'm saying in that is, one year old, you get a birthday and after that there's no more. The next biggest event on the island is death. When a person dies the bigger pig you bring to the funeral, the more honor you're paying this individual. Those are the two biggest events that happen on the island. One other very unusual custom that I found is their judicial branch of government. It's tribal, some common law, the other. By that, one example I mean is if I kill someone on the island, I murdered them and this person's family decides to forgive me and adopt me as their own son, there's nothing in the law that can put me in prison or can even arrest me. If the family's willing to forgive me and adopt me as their own son, Another custom that was real hard to get used to is if you tell someone that you'll be there at twelve o'clock, to a Pohnpein, that could be twelve o'clock tomorrow, twelve o'clock the next day or twelve o'clock next week. They will tell you anything that you want to know because in their culture you never can tell anybody no. You just don't just don't show up.

POHNPEI SPEAKS FIVE TONGUES

On Pohnpei five languages are spoken. In Micronesia each island state has a different culture and language. English is the Nation's language but each speakers their own on their own island so when you bring all these islands together with English being everybody's second, you have the making of a fruitbasket turnover.

Also I want you to know that some of the islands had been at war with each other for hundreds of years so when you put them together in a government, trouble will happen. It's like North, South, the War has been over since 1865 but it's still with us today.

SURPRISE!

The breast in Pohnpei is only for child-rearing so about my second week, I was walking up a path to school and a young girl about 14 years old came running by me and she was topless. I said, "Good gosh almighty." because I hadn't had too many times in my life to see that, so I liked. I'm only human. After about two weeks, you get used to it as every day life, but a woman will never show anything above the knee.

PEACE CORPS SEND A PACKAGE

Before I left for Micronesia, Peace Corps sent me a package about knight-crawling. That is the way a boy meets a girl on Pohnpei. The package said to take a box of Spam. Use an ice pick to punch holes in it and at night when you go knight-crawling, throw the Spam out so you can get the dogs fighting each other so that you can tap on the girl's door. When the girl comes out, you don't talk. You just have sex. Wham, Bam, Thank you Ma'am, it's over. Boys and girls never speak to each other during the day but a third party will arrange for a meeting to take place, but it's all done in secret.

KNIGHT CRAWLING

I heard of an American trying this. He was about 21 years old, blond headed which the people love. He had tapped on a few doors and had a good success rate until he went after a girl whose father had a high title and you don't mess with those girls. It's sorta like when you were a boy trying to look up dress of a hoop dress of a Southern Belle. You just don't do it. Anyway, the guy wouldn't listen to two different warning the family had sent him, so one night he went crawling and he tapped on the door but behind the bushes her father and brother took a big knife across the arm of the boy. He never went crawling again and left for the states.

BOYS GET AN EDUCATION

A girl can marry on Pohnpei at the age of 14. As soon as a boy thinks he can do anything sexual, he tries. It's at funerals when they're free from their parents that the boys start knight crawling. Usually they're junior high boys and the girls are mich older and not married for some reason. The older girl spots the boy. He becomes submissive and the girl pulls his pants down and she gets on top of him and they have sex. No talking, they don't even know each other's name.

When it's or they both go separate ways. I had been left many times about a moral decision. Do you tell them it's right or wrong. If they're Catholic they don't believe in birth control which 50% of the island is. I would never tell a boy that sex is a sin but I would say that he is too young to have a child so give them the birth control device.

If the girl has a child it becomes the responsibility of the girl's father or oldest brother to take care of it.

Pohnpeins look at sex as natural, a very strong need that has to be fulfilled after food and shelter, where as for example, In Alabama, you can't even buy a Playboy because of the churches saying it's something wrong or dirty about sex. When in Alabama you have the highest teenage birth rate of any state in the Union so somebody is doing something.

The first time a boy masturbates and sperm comes out, then he goes and tells his father the next day about this great event. The father is so happy because it mans he will have grandchildren. It's a coming of age thing and they both go out together and plant a yam together.

4

SCHOOL-EDUCATION

Their education is just like ours, set up exactly the same as ours is, with a few exceptions. The older people on the island consider an education for their kids is how good they can use a machete because that's their survival, the machete. Also, they want them to learn how to plant yams. When a boy reaches the age of twelve or thirteen or fourteen—the biggest event that he and his father will share together is the planting of yams. They leave the yams in four one year, come back, and some times those yams weigh up to one hundred pounds. But a kid's education as we see it is not maybe the priority that you would think. Sometimes the kids would be out of school, would not enter school until they were ten, eleven or maybe twelve. So it was nothing unusual to have a sixth grader who was sixteen years old. It's mandatory on the island but it's not enforced, that everybody goes to an elementary school from the first through the eighth grade. They have one public high school on the island. The government allows for only thirty-seven per cent of the students to go to this high school, only thirty-seven per cent. How do they go? They take a test in English and math. Remember English is their second language and Pohnpein is their first. They have a State Department of Educatio, with a State Department Head, deputy superintendent and so forth. What was so unusual about this was they have specialists for everything and anything that you can come up with. The other schools that are on the islands are a vocational school, several small church school and a college prep school for those located in Truk, I'll talk more about that later on.

MY SCHOOL, NETT

Nett—We had over six hundred students. We were the largest municipality of the rural schools on the islands. My principal's name was Maria. Maria was not your typical Pchnpein woman. She was very outspoken, very strong-willed woman. She reminded me a lot of the way Margaret Thatcher runs her government. It's pretty well her way or no way and that's very unusual for her to be a supervisor over a bunch of men in school, which consisted of eighteen teachers and three aids. Very unusual in Pohnpei. But I had the greatest amount of respect for her. We had our disagreements but Maria and I could always agree on one thing and that was the best interests of the students came before me or her either one. So that was our biggest thing that we had working together. Most of the teachers at my school had had a year of college or more, most had come to America and went to school here but only stayed for a year or two. The biggest thing that they worked for was an Associate of Arts degree. When I reached my school in Nett, most of my students couldn't even affort a pencil, paper or anything. One shirt a year was all they had. The school rooms were wife open, with a fence at the top like wire, no electricity, no air-conditioning and when it rained, if it rained hard and the river got up, then the students had to stay at the school or somewhere else. They walked to school every day just like I did. The lunch room was run by the food service program in the United States, that's one of their social program the United States has given them—Pohnpein students. Also one good thing about their school lunch program is the United States gives them money so they can buy local food to feed the students and that helps their economy.

MY CLASSROOM

There are no books to be mentioned on the island. My principal, bless her heart, she had about twenty McMillan English books, from a Catholic school that closed down on the island. So seventh grade and the eighth grade used those same books. I had three classes to teach, two eighth grade classes which was about seventh-seven to eighty students, one seventh grade class which was fifty students. My principal said, when I went there, that she didn't care how I taught all she wanted was a few goals. I asked, "What are they?" She said, "One, I want my students to speak English, two, I want them to be able stand up in front of a group of people and speak English." That's what I did. We had a book but it was all set up for British English and my principal didn't like it, and I didn't like it, so I didn't use it. One of the first things that I went to go when I started my classroom was, I had to build up their self-esteem about themselves, their culture, but also I had to improve their education so that they could further their education, because they have the same citizenship rights to go to American school as we do. I had a conflict of interest in this that I had to really stress their culture because they needed to have heir own language and their own culture to be very vital and very important, in fact, more important than English because unless they have that self-esteem about their culture and their people they would never succeed in anything else. So, that was my first priority.

METHODS

One of the first things that I had my students do was to keep a journal, write three entries a week. I would bring outside pictures into the class, the reading materials that I got from the states and remember, there are no newspapers on the island, no television so anything that I brought to them was more than they had to begin with. I let them look at the pictures and I found that most of the time in the pictures, usually the National Enquirer and the National Star had such beautiful pictures the students could use their imaginations to write about them. I had a time trying to convince them that everything they read wasn't literally true. I would let them build vocabulary words. Antonyms, synonyms, homonyms, let them write down meanings, sentences, spelling, about four different times during one week so that I would make sure that they would learn the word. I had them writing essays on many subjects. their lives, their culture, their families, their wants, their needs, their hopes and the main thing in all of this was to have them stand up in front of the class and speak English. They did very well. One of the lessons that I found to be interesting was, I would let three or four of the students come in front of the class, and they would pretend that they were the governor or it. Governor or president or whatever and let the students ask them questions and let them solve the problems of their own nation.

SPEAKING ENGLISH

Most of the time I would come into my classroom I would sit or stand, ask my students different questions and they would ask me different questions. I would ask them what kinds of food they liked to eat. Most would say rice or they didn't like rice because that's what they eat all the time. Subjects in school—what did they like, what did they have plans for after school? I would ask them questions like that. What was their favorite video? Most of the time was always Rambo. They would ask me questions like "Why did America kill President Kennedy?" Remember there are no newspapers, no TV anywhere. President Kennedy was loved on that island and they knew about him, but not many other American presidents. They would ask why did Americans have slaves? Why was I so big, my mother's name and my father's name. One of the things that I also did in my class was, along with talking in English I had them write pen-pal letters back to the States. By them writing to the States it was the first time that they'd ever received any mail from overseas. But the comparison between the two students was this, my students on Pohnpei would talk about the beautiful landscape, flowers, orchids, waterfalls, just how beautiful everything is, their family going to a feast or whatever and the kids in Americas would about talk about how many cars they had, their stereos, their swimming pools and the friend of mine who did the go-between the letters in America asked one time, "Frank, do you think that your students feel guilty that they don't have as much as the kids in America do?" "No, they don't because they don't know what a swimming pool is, they don't know what a stereo system is, they know what cars are, they've seen enough videos to know that there are cars in America." So, you can see the difference in the two, one's talking about nature and the other is talking about materialistic things. I would have them stand up in class and read the letters. I could feel their self-esteem for them to see that American students, English being their first language, made mistakes, too They could see how they could read and write also. One of the funny things that we had in the pen-pal letters was my friend sent me a camera, a Polaroid camera with the films and I took pictures of the students and we exchanged pictures back and forth but what was so funny was to see my students, how they would wait and see a picture develope in front of their eyes, it was like magic to them.

SEGREGATED IN CLASS

Most of my classes, the boys would sit on one side, the girls sit on the other. The boys were aggressive, the girls were pacifists. They took a second seat to the boys. Girls would talk to me inside the classroom, but outside wouldn't say anything. Touching was very important. In their culture, if you liked someone, you'd touch them or you'd hold hands. That's between two people of the same sex. It's more important for you to have that relationship with your friends than it is for you to have your relationship with a wife or girlfriend, so touching was very important. Something I had to get used to myself.

FIGHTING IN CLASS

Overall I never had any trouble with any of my students, they were well-disciplined, well-behaved, very quiet. Every now and then something would flare up, and it happened one day. I was walking into the back and I heard plop, a slap, I turned around and this big girl slapped one of my male students. He slapped her back, they got into a fight. We broke them up and the girl lost control, she was a sixteen year old girl, a big girl, the other students never did like her, she was a bully and she was doing something that wasn't right in her culture. She was fighting a male, that sure wasn't right! I had to literally just <u>sit</u> <u>on</u> <u>her</u>. I didn't do anything to hurt her, but just sit on her, because if I didn't, she would have jumped on him again and I don't know what would have happened. Anyway that day at school they were giving out <u>worm</u> <u>treatments</u> to help the students, because that's a bad problem, and I sent the boy up there, his name was MacArthur. I let her up and as soon as I let her up, she went after him again. This was about 100 yards away and I had to wrestle her down again and sit on her and at this time I was begging and hollering for help from the staff and all to come help me but I was holding her down and we got them broke up. None of the staff ever came to help me and when I let her up again I sent the boy to the principal's office and she was on her way there and I saw she was going to jump on him again and I told one of the other students to step between and as doon ad he did. She wouldn't come at him because she knew if she came at him he would simply floor her without a question, because she was out of he place. But if I hadn't been real careful and real gentle with her, if I had hurt her in any way or humiliated her in front of her friends, her whole family would have come after me on the island with machetes, and I would have had leave for my own safety. So be being gentle with her while I was sitting on her and talking nice, softly, to her, I was able to let her save face and for me to be safe also. The year before the same thing had happened with the same girl student and she had so many family members and they weren't singing "Oh how I love Jesus."

REWARD SYSTEM

Something during class I would have the students do little games in front of the class, I would ask spelling words, and I had already given out numbers in class, like I through 20 and there would be another person in class who would have 20, two people would have 20. I would call out a word like <u>gum</u> or <u>run</u> or something and I would call out a number 20 and the students that rushed to the board the fastest and wrote the correct spelling would get a prize, which was usually bubble gum. That was quite a reward because most of my students never got to chew bubble gum. I used games like that all the time to motivate them.

CULTURAL EDUCATION

When a country or people lose their language, they lose their culture. When their culture is gone, everything is gone, because unless people feel identity with themselves and their past they have a very bad feeling about themselves. So, on Pohnpei they had what they called cultural teachers and after I finished up every day with my classes he would come behind and teach their word in Pohnpein to build up their vocabulary in their own language and also teach them about their culture and the old ways of doing things which is very important. The gentleman who was their cultural education teacher couldn't speak any English and I couldn't speak enough Pohnpein to have a conversation with him but we had a mutual respect for each other because he knew how important my job was and I knew how important his job was. He was a very tall man with white hair and when he smiled he reminded me of my grandfather back in the States.

GRADUATION

Graduation was the high point of my student's finishing up the eighth grade. For some it was one of the high points in their life. If they hadn't passed the high school test then the next high point was your first baby and getting married.

All my students had saved and bought a beautiful colorful flower looking shirt or dress for the girls that matched the boys. The ceremony started at 9:00. The stage looked like a Garden of Eden with fresh green shrubs and big gorgeous flowers.

The speeches went on and on. The longest was from the Congressman. The $30,000 a year man. Dressed like a million dollars. He was going to give out two scholarships. One to the vocational school and the other to the Jesuit school on Truk. One year pay was not more than $300.00 but he had to tell the people how much he cared about them or that's what someone told me he said. The speeches finally ended and then my students got 15 minutes of the program. Five minutes of that was singing "Shall we Gather at the River."

As my students left the stage, they lined up behind a row of flowers, blue, red, white, etc. All kinds waiting to be congratulated by everybody. Men don't cry but I sure did. It was like I lost my family, 76 boys and girls. I did everything but lie, cheat, or steal for my students to have the best. I would often use one powerful person against another for my students to get the best. I pushed until I got my students at least a chance to swim instead of sinking in life before they even had a chance to get started.

Out of 76 students 70 passed. The government allowed for only 36% to pass the high school test. Well, the other six were low, very low so I paid $25.00 for summer school at the S. D. A. so that they could by pass the test and go on into the school for the fall. Whoever says can't beat the system is wrong. We did beat it and my students are swimming. Now it's up to them how far they swim.

ALABAMA

After I had been in Nett for some time, I wanted to know if they had ever heard of Alabama. To my shock my student had heard of Alabama even before I arrived. I asked how. They said, "In song." What song? "I come from Alabama with a banjo my knee." They all learned that song in earlier grades. "Do you know any more?" I asked. "Yes" they said. "What?" My home's in Alabama, Southern born and Southern bred.

5

BASKETBALL

You can ask the question, "Why would the Peace Corps send someone around the world to teach them basketball?" As the thing in basketball goes, the reason it was important in the Island and was my job, I guess you'd have to look at my background as to why I was successful there. because there are so many youth in the Island, there's nothing for them to do. Keeping them active keeps the crime rate down. My background in basketball goes back many years. The first game that I was supposed to coach in, we lost 34 to 4, would have lost by more than that but the referee was one-sided towards us after it was such a lopsided victory. This was little boys, first grade through sixth grade. I was supposed to help the guy coach but he didn't show up, so I went by myself and after the ballgame when we got beat, I went to a friend's house, because I took it so seriously and I said, "I've got to be the worst basketball coach that's ever been in the world." I couldn't help but cry because I felt so bad. He said, "No, you're not, just give it time." So, I said, "Well, I'll learn, then won't nobody else beat me this way." I coached basketball at Boys' Club, YMCA, and different churches. When you coach basketball in your churches, while working in a church it's like working in a third world country, you don't get any <u>support</u>, <u>encouragement</u> or <u>help</u>. The last church I volunteered with youth, at my church we had 1,400 members and I couldn't get people to help me so I ended up coaching four basketball teams while working forty hours a week. They never tell you thank you, they never give you any praise. You can go pick them up, you can carry them home, you can spend hours practicing ball after you finish your work, you can spend your weekends coaching, you can spend your hours on he telephone trying to get places to practice, and still nobody ever thanks you. My background in basketball has really helped me in the Peace Corps. By the way, my record before I left the States to join the Peace Corps, in basketball, the last two years, the six teams that I coached, was 59 wins, 11 losses. I had a secret to that—when I coached my ball players I would find their strong points and work on their strong points, and work with them in practice and I could feel and sense the way the looked and talked or acted, how much they were putting out or what they were feeling, how far they needed to go, to encouragement or anything. I constantly worked on positive reinforcement, never used negative reinforcement. That's talking a lot of boys who otherwise would never get a chance to play, to play on my team and participate. I was real happy that I could let everybody plan and we still won a lot of ballgames. Getting back to the education in basketball, how the two worked together, I taught school twenty hours a week, English, from eight o'clock to eleven thirty.

When I went to my village in September, I started right away trying to get the education department to get a basketball league started. I started in September and it was December. What I would do, I would go and talk, it took me one hour to walk into town, one solid hour and each week I would go in and I would talk to this specialist, next week, he would say, "Well, I can't make a decision, go talk to this guy." Then come back to this one, and it just went on and on. All this time I'm trying to get this league started with education. I'm having to put up with elements, rain sometimes seven inches a day, the humidity and you've got to walk everywhere you go. That part is the real tough part. I wanted a basketball program, I said that I was going to get it. I wasn't going to stop until I got one. I believe if you won't be beat then you can't be beat. That's exactly what I did. I started, as I said, in September, one day a week I'd go into town and try to get this basketball league started and as I said before, they sent you every place that you could go. I went to see Josh, he was our host agency, youth affairs, saw Lewis, he was an education PE specialist, just called himself a specialist, the principal of a school, the only public school on the Island, and Larilyn, she was another Peace Corps volunteer. She couldn't do the things I could do but without her encouragement we would have never got it off the ground. We met and talked about it, we thought for awhile we were going to have to play on a court outside, and I knew what the rain situation would be. There were two inside gymnasiums on the island. We had the meeting and in their culture, everything is expected to fall, it's very common to criticize everything and everybody. I was real scared that Lewis was against it and he was against it all the way through and I never knew why. Maybe it was because a foreigner like myself was getting the idea up. Anyway, after we had the season, Lewis took credit that he founded it. We had a meeting that day and we talked about it and really the meeting had no bearing on how the league finally got started, but it did, at least I say it did. In December, I went by to see Josh again and he had received a call from these men and they said that we weren't going to have a basketball league. They accept failure in a third world country as an everyday occurrence, it happens so much. I had been working on this basketball league since September and walking and getting headaches and one of the few times in my life I used bad words but I told John, "We're damn sure going to have a basketball league and we're going to put some fire under some asses." By saying that I got his attention. I didn't use that method until the end of it, because we are to help and let them lead. But it just wasn't going anywhere and I knew that if it was to get started I had to take the bull by the horns and go with it, so that's what I did. We were supposed to play outside, luckily enough a former Peace Corps volunteer had returned to the Island who working on a Sports' Council and when he came in, Jim Tobin, it was quite a help, for him to come in and help us further our program. Once we got it set up to start, also between September and December, I was holding basketball clinics around the Island. I would load up and carry my basketball and put my backpack on my back and my umbrella and hitchhike to another village to teach the locals about basketball. This one guy I was going to teach about basketball was named James, and we were working there one day together by ourselves and I was teaching James about basketball. I was showing him something, a pivot and then he would do the same thing, then tell me in English and all of a sudden James started to cry. In their culture, men don't cry. I said, "James, what's wrong?" I reached over and put my arm around him and he said he was sorry but he couldn't understand English. I said we'll figure that out. I said, "I'll show you what to do, and then you tell me in your language, Pohnpein, what I'm doing. I said, "Come on James, you tell me in Pohnpein what you want me to know, tell me in Pohnpein what I'm doing so you can relate it to your ball players, and he did and it worked real good and I developed a friend in him that stayed with me the rest of my stay on the Island. The other clinic that I had was with my host father, his name title was Karom, that was his village name, Karom. Remember that I mentioned that in their culture you didn't tell anybody everything that you knew. Well, Karom was always skeptical and scared that I wouldn't tell him all that I know, but I was doing the best that I could considering that the boys had never seen the game on television much less in person, because I introduced it and it was all new. Karom was doing a real good job and I moved a little farther toward the first of the season and Karom went up against two of my ball teams and he defeated them by two points and by one point and he still came up to me and told me that I didn't tell him all that I know, and he'd beaten me. That was an interesting experience.

SPORTSMANSHIP CLASS

Well, the biggest mistake I made was putting two sixth graders on my eight grade A team. The reason was one was 17 years old and the other was 14. I needed my butt kicked for doing that. They are so rude! Never do what I asked them. I talked to them and they look away in the top of the building but for some weird reason the eighth grade A team boys thinks they are super when they play only for themselves and never as a teem. We got beat by another team and after the game the oldest wanted to start a fight with a bench warmer who never plays and is very small. He doesn't go after the big guys, he goes after the smallest. It made me very angry. It just shows me he is a coward. In the hundreds of boys I've coached, I've never had two get on my nerves as bad as these two did but then if they cared anything about an education and different attitude, they could have started on any high school in America and higher.

After every game win, lose, or drew, I would have them go over and shake hands with every player on the other side even if I had to drag them on the floor, they were going have class. I only had to drag one but he fought me every step of the way.

I never would cheat but I sometimes did things to give us an edge like bring a pair of fingernail clippers and have the referee clip the nails of the other side. Make them take off watches, rings, etc. but to a teen that can be a damaging blow to lose that good luck charm.

I might even yell so loud that the other team would look at me in fear. If my team won, "we won", if we lost, "I lost." After the game I would be so tired, my heart wouldn't stop beating so fast I couldn't sleep.

I knew every boy. His strong and weak points. I would push him until he gave it his all. If he felt like crying, I would just hold him. I let his teammates choose the rules, not me. They were always harder than I could ever be. Some of the boys were so bad that we almost lost the game because we were trying to let him score. It would be 3 or 4 guys on this one little player to keep him from scoring. I want them to feel part of a group, a team. Have good memories to look back on when life sometimes gives you a raw deal and I think I did.

MY TEAM

Sixth, seventh and eighth grade boys, eighty boys all together, four teams, 20 boys on a team. We practiced four times a week, one team at a time, you have to remember that I'm teaching boys who have never seen a basketball game on TV in their life, they didn't know Larry Bard and Moses Malone and their English wasn't too good and I'm teaching them on a half of a basketball court, that a Cat Team built on the Island. I had that to contend with, we did that four times a week from September until December. We had the heat to contend with and the humidity just about did me in. The biggest trouble I had was with the youth that were not at my school. Why did I have trouble with them? One, the government only allows thirty-seven percent of the students to enter high school and if you're not one of them and you're left with only an eighth grade education and don't have anywhere to go, you don't have a trade or any skills to learn an occupation, you're really dead. Your world comes to an end. The older boys just couldn't stand seeing the Nett school boys playing together part of a group and most of all they couldn't stand seeing my boys feeling good about themselves. They are also feeling bad because of their culture. They were a food gathering culture and all of a sudden America has come in and every American they see has money to buy nice clothes and watches and good food and drive the rent-a-cars and the Pohnpein men just can't compete. It's hard on them between the classes, the two cultures that they're facing now, and another thing is alcoholism is real bad among the youth. One thing that you sort of overlook is when they think of Americans is when an American male comes over, the Pohnpein women throw themselves on the men because they look at it as a way to go to America, everyone of them wants to go to America. The males have this built-in hatred for all American males. My trouble that I had with the youths was five different times at nighttime they'd come out on the court and tore my basketball rims down, literally tore them out of the sockets, left them hanging. They would make fun of me and harrass me and yell while I was trying to teach, sometimes throw rocks at me and I was scared, I was scared, I have to admit that, many times, but I didn't show any fear or aggressiveness. Those two things kept me safe from the youth that were having the trouble, but at the last of it it got so bad that they were coming down on the court and harassing my students and me too. It was a scene for some ugly confrontations. At that time my principal decided for the best interest of me and the school, to stop practicing so we stopped practicing in December.

When we got the league started in January, toward the end of January, my boys hadn't practiced any up until then, but before we go any further, I'd like to say that we had nineteen teams in two different leagues which I founded, so that left me real busy with my boys. "Well, I couldn't practice anymore at my court, in my municipality, so I said, I'm going to try somewhere else." There's not too many places to practice, and I needed to practice. What I did was go to the little community college there, in town. I used my Principal's influence to get us a place to practice. This guy who's in charge of the college wants to be Governor and the only way you can be Governor is have a lot of people like you. My principal's hundred was in the State Legislature, so I really used that, otherwise, I would never have got a chance to use the gymnasium to play. It's not like what you'd call a gymnasium, it cost $31,000,00 to build, has a concrete floor, a top over it. and concrete up maybe four foot high, and the rest of it is screen wire, it's not exactly what you'd look as our gymnasiums and there are no bleachers or anything in it, marked off real good. A real nice place to practice so on Sunday afternoons, the boys and I would practice basketball there. One thing I found out quickly, in their culture, is to share, so after practice every day I would have a big drink, a 32 ounce Coke, or something, and we would share it. While we were sharing it, I would drink the first and they would drink the rest. That was quite a treat for the boys because some had never tasted a Coke. It was also a way for me to rally blend in with their culture. It was tremendously hard teaching that many boys the basics of basketball. One of my main goals in Peace Corps was to teach the locals how to do this. While I was practicing at school all the local teachers would sit and watch but they wouldn't come out to help me. I wanted their help, but I couldn't get it and so I went ahead and did it myself. Toward the end of it I had four teachers who got to be real good coaches, who were helping me, only at the games, but they wouldn't practice. They never helped me practice, well one would, but the others never did help me to practice. We started the league with nineteen teams, two league, and probably eight or nine hundred boys.

The first real hard basketball game that I remember there took place in February, it was one of my eighth grade teams going against SDA. SDA stood for Seventh Day Adventist, they have a good Church school on the Island. The difference between them and us was they had their own gym to practice and we didn't. They required their students to practice one hour a day, five days a week and with four teams and thirty boys on each team, I wasn't able to equal what SDA had. They had only fifteen boys and a place to practice every day. It was like the rich side of town playing the poor side of town, is the way I would look at these two. We were playing at their gymnasium, SDA, the crowd was a big factor, but my boys were ready. I was so proud of them all. We played such a good game even up to eighteen seconds left, we were so close to winning. Their coach just bragged on us and told us what a good job we had done. My players were so down, one of my players came by and I looked at him and grabbed him and he was about to cry, and I was about to cry, and you didn't do that in their society. I gave him a big hug and told him I was proud of him and I loved him regardless of how the game had come out. What was so unusual about the game at SDA was my boys were going in their playing, and you would think that they were playing at the Superdome in New Orleans, it just scared them to death.

One of the next big games that I remember wasn't one of my teams. It was a game that another Peace Corps volunteer that I had trained coached. He had his own basketball team, and he was playing in his first game that he had coached. This was in January. He was coaching against a man on the other side of the Island named Bill. Bill had been a professional coach before he became a Missionary. So, Bill knew what he was doing. Bryan brought his team out, he didn't even have a basketball court to practice on, he did the best he could with nothing. Bill's team beat him seventy-four to two. The worst humiliation I'd ever seen in a basketball game in my life. In their culture it's more important to tie than to win as a group and his team had won 74-2. I was angry ay this, I couldn't help but cry, I felt so sorry for the boys. They lost face, they couldn't go back to their village and hold their heads up at school, at time, at church, or anywhere. I knew how bad they felt, they loaded up on the back of the truck and one little boy grabbed my hand and squeezed my hand. It was like squeezing a feeling of security on his part. I told the boys, "If I can get my boys relaxed, we'll make Bill's day uncomfortable." I met Bill at Church later on and we had some quiet disagreement over his style of coaching and my style of coaching. I don't believe in beating someone that bad and he thought he was teaching the boys bad skills if thy went into a stall. We had some bad disagreements over that but after a few weeks he changed his style and changed the way he was playing and bill and I became real good friends. I think he's a very fine man goday. I'm really happy he is my friend.

TRIP TO BRYAN

I felt so sorry for Bryan losing 74-2 that I offered to help him out that coming Sunday if he would get a family member to pick me up because I didn't want to walk 3 hours. Anyway the guy picked me up and I met Bryan, 6'3", 130 1bs, white headed and looks just like "Andrew Jackson." Bryan didn't have a court so I sued sticks to make a court. We had about 4 hours of good practice and it was dark before I knew it. I loved helping out Bryan and his boys but I knew it was past 5:00 and the drunks were coming out. I can not stand to be around drinking! Anyway, Bryan got his Pohnpein brother to drive us who had had a fight with his girl friend and was drunk which I didn't look at the driver as I usually do to see if he is drunk which was my mistake. That guy cleaned out ditches, running kids, hogs, dogs for cover. Me and Bryan was holding on for dear life. I said "Oh, God, don't let me die like this." Somehow we made it o.k. I did my best to talk Bryan out of riding with him but I had no luck. Bryan made it back o.k. by sitting in the truck talking to him to slow down and take it easy.

TO MEET THE GOVERNOR

One day after a basketball game my team had lost, a small hand touched me on the shoulder. It was a young boy of 13 or 14. He said that I was a wonderful coach and he gave me a cold coke and boy it was good, the coke and the encouragement. The boy was tall for a Pohnpein. His hair was blond and his skin an olive red color. He started asking me if I had ever been to Disneyworld. I said yes and I asked him his name. He said, "Esmond Moses", the Governor's son, "yes." I met Governor Moses at a later time. He was my third Governor that I had met. The first being George Wallace of Alabama and after he was shot I met Governor Jimmy Carter, of Georgia who had come to Alabama to help raise money for Governor Wallace's hospital bill in Maryland in 1972.

I really wanted to see Governor Moses' house. I just knew that it was like Marcos' home in the Philippines but it wasn't. It was a nice house on Pohnpei but it wouldn't be in the States. I guess in Alabama it would sell for $40,000.

Governor Moses was short in stature. His eyes had a sparkle in them. He was thinning on top just a little. Some said he used to work for former Sec. of State Henry Kissinger. His wife was very tall. She was a very attractive lady with blond hair.

I never knew them too well but everybody on the Island loved them. He has a very hard job on Pohnpei as the Governor but I think he was doing his best.

I was coaching four times a week plus teaching twenty hours a week. After the second week I was totally exhausted. The games were some so close, some not, we won but the hardest thing was dealing with the boys. When they lost it was really a tremendous blow. You would have thought the world had come to an end. I'd never had to build up boys as hard as I had to build these up. When they lost it was just the end of life and already their self-esteem was at a record low. But we made it through. My basketball teams that met in elementary school won twenty-four times, lost nine, that's including sixth graders, seventh graders, two eighth graders playing against everybody on the Island. I was very proud, very happy. It was an exhausting time for me whenever the teams would lose, and they did at times, I couldn't sleep at night, my heart rate would be so fast, I was totally exhausted. It was really hard to take, I took every loss to heart. I was wondering at one time if I'd ever beat another American coach, there were a few on the Island. All of the frustration, the downs, the lows, along with being away from home is just real tough to bear.

What the boys had learned from this as I did in my coaching, I built up players to do the best they can. I don't break down players I grab them by the hand and help them up instead of beating them down. I never jump on them, I never criticize them. If I have to get firm with one of hem I will, but when I do I put out a hand to give him strength and support to build him back up. If one of them makes a mistake, I quickly take him and put my arm around him and many times I told them I loved and cared about them and I wouldn't be there if I didn't.

I used only two methods. Coach Bear Bryant always said that you care about your players as human beings and work to make them the best human being that they can be. Second, you always be willing to change. For example, long hair in he States, earrings, on Pohnpei it was putting different colored finger nail polish on each hand. I always knew I wasn't the smartest or best coach. I just worked longer and harder than anyone else.

6

STUDENTS BODIES

I'm 6'3" tall and weigh 240 1bs. That is big for the States but on Pohnpei I was the biggest person on the Island of 21,000 people so when I went to school all the kids were scare of me. They didn't know if I was a good or bad giant so it just happened that I brought with me about 200 combs and I gave them out. You see kindness worked because they started getting close to me.

I have a lot of body hair and the students had never seen anybody who had hair except on their head so they loved to told my hand and rub their fingers over my arms.

Pohnpein men and boys have beautiful bodies. Deep brown, well cut up like a body builder, short in height and no body hair. Even the men who are in their 40's have no love handles on the side. I wish the secret to that one.

Pohnpein girls are beautiful when they're young but as they get older they eat and eat until they're <u>fat</u> <u>little</u> <u>women</u>. Fat women are considered beautiful on Pohnpei! A girl or woman who is slim is looked down on by everybody.

STUDENTS

<u>MARIO</u>—One day in school I had my students write down a person that they really admired and respected. Mario got up in front of the class and he started talking about how much he admired and respected me. How I was one of the few adults who gave their word and kept it. It just floored me, to hear him say those nice things about me. Right away I was scared that the other students would pick on him, because he did say that. Mario's background—His father died when was a baby, his mother, he doesn't even consider her his mother, she's an alcoholic. I guess the way that I really got close to Mario is when one day in the classroom, he and a girl student had words and the Principal was looking to suspend Mario and I steped in and said, "Please don't." I took Mario off to the side and said, "Mario, please don't say bad words to this girls, because they'll kick you out of school if you do." Then he started talking to me, this is really where we got close.

One day Mario was walking up the road when he heard some of the teenagers that had given me such a hard time saying bad things about me. Not necessary me as a person but as an American. Mario told them to stop saying these bad things so they jumped on Mario and kicked him in the stomach and the groin bruised his ribs face, his eyes, his lips real bad. He told me about and I was totally humbled and shocked. I had never had anybody in my life take a beating for me. At Christmas time I bought Mario a watch and he was one of the most loyal students that I ever had.

Mario's dream at that time was to go to the vocational school on the Island to get an education and to have three meals a day to eat and to have a bed to sleep in at night. Mario got his wish before I left the Island. I was able, with the help of the Principal to get him enrolled in this school. He was luckly enough that Legislature on the Island paid his way. So Mario got his dream come true.

Wilson—When I first got there, Wilson didn't like me, period. He gave me a lot of trouble in class. Wilson's skin color was as white as a sheet of paper. That was because of his Spanish background. He was one of the boys who had jumped on Mario, beat him up. He was always giving someday a bad go of it. I never put Wilson down, he was playing on the basketball team, we got beat one day and he walked off instead of staying when the game was over, so the boys voted him off the team. I intervened and gave the boys a chance to vote him back on the team, otherwise that was the end of his playing days. So he respected me for that and at Christmas time I bought him a shirt and slowly he began to come around and he would talk to me but not much. But before I left I would see him on the road and he would come and shake hands with me, which made me feel real good.

CEASAR—Ceasar was, I guess, fourteen, cutest little guy you ever wanted to look at. You could see that there was Spanish blood in him. The way I got to know Ceasar was, well he came to live with my family. While he was living with my family, he was outside with the girls and the oldest girl got mad with him for some reason and jumped on him and bit a bad place out on his neck. Ceasar couldn't defend himself because the girl's father is older than his Mother, real complicated there. But in that case Ceasar could not defend himself.

He came down with me and I looked at the bite and cleaned it up and bandaged it and got myself a little buddy. Everywhere I went, he went. He could speak good English. We went on a picnic and he cooked me a hotdog, and would do all kinds of little things. It was real funny, when we went on one picnic out to the ocean, on the beach, he said that his family clan member was the shark and if the shark came up, the shark would not eat him. I was glad no shark came up because I did not want to see Ceasar jumping into the water to see if the shark would eat him. At night he was always there to sleep with me because it wasn't good to be by yourself.

SELENE—The next student that I want to talk about is a girl named Selene. I guess she was sixteen or seventeen. She was a beautiful girl, skin real rosy red. You could see the Japanese in her eyes, from when the Japanese were there. Selene had long black hair and was not your typical Pohnpein girl, she would come up to me and talk to me, and tell me about her dreams about coming to california and working as a secretary. She'd tell me all kinds of things. She was doing things that were not culturally accepted. I got real close to her and toward the end of school, I had read in her journal that she had failed the test and she was so low. As I have mentioned before, they had a Seventh Day Adventist School and a man in the States had sent me some money that he owed me, so I paid for her to go to Summer School, which I think, was $25.00, a lot of money for over there. I sent her there and her father came and thanked me and I've never been thanked so much by a person in my whole life as he thanked me. He was going to bring me yam and taro and any other thing he had, because of my kindness to his daughter. It never was mentioned, but I had a strong sense of feeling that he wanted me to be his son-in-law. I think that was one of his goals.

BRITALINO—The next student that I want to mention is Britalino. He was a sixteen year old boy. His skin was real dark, he was a big boy for a Pohnpein but had leadership skills as good as any I've ever seen. He was not your typical Pohnpein, where they tell you what they want you to hear but his father was dying and I didn't know what to do but I wanted to do something. You don't send cards over there. So I asked another student, What could I do? I was going through a third party, what you should do, and he said his father liked eggs, so I went and bought two dozen eggs and gave them to him and his whole family, Britalino's whole family wrote me a thank you letter and told me how much that meant for me to give their father those eggs before he died. He said that I was the only white man who ever did anything good for him.

One day I was walking back toward my place, home, and feeling real low and Britalino came up and shook my hand which every time you meet someone you shake their hand, you usually hold their hand if you walk and he told me to please not to leave to come back to America that he really wanted me to stay and watch him graduate from elementary school and how much it meant to him for me to stay there. Him doing that was really an instrument to me, seek word of encouragement. He passed the test so he is going to one of the schools, the public school on the Island. He also has a brother in Texas so I'll see him one day.

<u>WEDGINER</u>—The next little guy I want to mention is called Wedginer. Wedginer was the littlest guy you wanted to look at, cute as he could be, little black-headed, real black all over, hair is straight, smiles, giggles cute grin. In January, he got up in front of the class to read his pen pal letter, while he was up there the other class members laughed at him, because you see, his family didn't come from a high village background. by that I mean they didn't have a high title so he wasn't treated that well. They made fun of him so I said well, I'm going to fix this, so that Saturday he and I went into town, a little old town there, we went to this one place that had a video in their little restaurant. we would go rent a movie and eat ice cream. He'd never done that before. When his birthday came up, we went into town again. When I'm saying going into town, that's one solid hours walk. We walked in there and there were about three stores that you could pick from in shoes so we went to all three of them and I said to him, okay, pick the pair you want and he said how much money you got and I said about fourteen dollars so he picked the pair he wanted. Before I left I was on the other side of the Island and he heard that I was leaving and he walked about fourteen miles to see me off at the airport. He called me Dad and Wedginer's ambition is to come to live with me in America. I hope to fulfill that dream one day. He wrote me a letter the other day and his letter said, he called me Dad as usual, which is pretty hard for me to get used to, he said his uncle was out swimming in the ocean and a shark came up and ate him. So what I'm going to do now is to look to helping him get through Summer School. I don't know if he'll pass the test or not but he's one of my top priorities to look after.

<u>BRADLEY</u>—Bradley had heard about the miracle cure "Ben-Gay" and he showed up at my door one night and wanted some on his thigh because it hurt. He dropped his pants and I started rubbing it all over his thigh and knee. Gosh, did those boys love that "Ben-Gay." Anyway Bradley started telling me about his stop-mother taking scissors and cutting up a shirt that his mother sent to him. The guy was small, deep black eyes and believed in himself about as much as a prison inmate and the cause of that was his step-mother making him feel like he was nothing with which I could identify. Anyway he started crying. He cried and cried. I held him and he cried on my shoulder. I had known someone who knew his mother on another Island so I said Bradley, you want to write your mother. He said YES. He was so happy so I helped him write her a letter. I sent the letter and within days I had a reply. I was already putting myself in harms way by the letter. The mother wanted me to tell his family that I was taking Bradley off the Island for a vacation and bring him to her. <u>Kidnapping that is</u>! Well, I had done

my part now and Bradley had her address so I wasn't going to do any kidnapping for anybody.

7

STUDENTS LETTERS

Dear Frank

Frank, we got your letter on September 2/89. I read the letter to the whole family. Everybody were glad to hear from you.

Here in Pohnpei, there is no news that you need to know now, Pohnpei is developing but ~~slowly~~, slowly.

In your Pohnpeian family you are still my son, Frank, Frank this summer I worked with Peace Group P/C at Palikir. The trainee ~~was~~ was at Palikir Elementry School.

I enjoyed working with them, ~~about~~ teacher.

Frank Ringlen is in high school at Seven Day Church High School. Do you remember the school we used to go and played Basket ball at theirs cord, that the school he is in.

Frank thank for the watches you sent.

Frank, say ~~hello~~ hollow to you mam, and everybody in your family.

Good by Frank we miss you, Halvorsen Kaprie

My Host Father

40

POHNPEI SPORTS COUNCIL

P. O. BOX 72
KOLONIA, POHNPEI 96941
FEDERATED STATES OF MICRONESIA

PRESIDENT
Lee Mendiola

VICE-PRESIDENT
Ewalt Joseph

TREASURER
Bethwel Henry

SECRETARY
Mohner Esiel

MEMBERS
Saburo Max
Walter Simiram
Kun Isaac

RECREATION SPECIALISTS
Methos Edward
Nimrod Half

ADMINISTRATOR
Jim Tobin

April 6, 1987

The Honorable Resio S. Moses
Governor
Pohnpei State
Kolonia, Pohnpei 96941

Dear Governor:

The first annual Pohnpei boy's youth basketball league concluded last week with a championship tournament. The league began in January, with 19 teams participating from elementary schools around Pohnpei. The results were:

          1st - Sekere A
          2nd - Awak
          3rd - Sekere B
          4th - SDA
          5th - Nett C

The league was coordinated by the Sports Council, which provided rules, schedules, equipments, game officials, gymnasium rental fees and trophies. The teams did not pay a registration fee. Only adult teams are charged fees.

Frank Burkett and Larylin Pittman, Peace Corps Volunteers, were instrumental in organizing the league, and later coached teams. We would like to thank them and the other PCV coaches who did outstanding jobs:

          Jim Cope - Wapar
          Bonnie Ketcham - Sokehs Powe
          Brian Ahern - Saladak
          Frank Burkett - Nett
          Larylin Pittman - Paliker

With help from Peace Corps and Youth Affairs a year round sports program for the elementary school aged youth will be implimented. The sports will be: basketball, volleyball, softball, soccer, baseball (Little League and up) and track and field. Girls' softball has already started (12 teams) and boys' volleyball (18 teams) will start next week.

Sincerely yours,

Jim Tobin

cc: Speaker, Pohnpei Legislature
     Director, Education
     Director, Peace Corps FSM
     Peace Corps Volunteer Coaches

Jordan Gallen
P.O. Box 309
Kolonia, Pohnpei FSM 96941

Dear Frank,   Write back to me.

     Hi Frank. How are you. I would like to
thank you for your kindness. I also want to
thank you for helping me. I was very happy
when we went to the hospital. I want you
to know that I learn a lot in Oral English. The
new words you taught us are very good.
I felt good! when you shook my hand and
said that I did a good job. I really enjoyed
the wrestling books. You always polite to me.
I am glad that you come to Nett. I
will stop here because I am busy. Good-bye.
May God bless you.

                    Your friend
                    big Jordan

Pohnpei Students

Po. Box 1553
Kolohnia Pohnpei FSM #96911
Dec. 17, 1986

Dear Mr. Burkett
Hello there before proceeding down, I would like to thank to our heavenly father for his real kindness of holding our lifes to now so that we can meet in this poor letter of mine. Hi how are you I hope that every thing is running smoothly with you. Sir Frank and I are best friend we are always get together to discuss things about education. He wants me to teach him about Pohnpeian languages and cultures. I wrote many languages and cultures and gave him yesterday.

Sir, you know Frank is a good man he is a very good teacher. He is an oral english teacher I learned more about English from him. He is a polite person. He is our basketball coach, All of my classmates and I love him. He always tell us try hard and won't give up. I love Frank so much because he is trying his best of teaching me in Oral english. sometimes I cry about him, because because I love him. Sir I'm sorry because I don't have much time this moment. I will end my letter here because I'm going to sleep. This time is 9:55 Frank gave me this watch because I won the Art contest, Okay there's not much to say laugh about these broken english. Good bye or God be with you. Have a nice Christmas

Faithfully yours
Mario Johnson

Dear Frank,

Hello again! How are you. Hope that you and your family had a fine holiday vacation. I've already received the card you send to me. I like it thank you very much.

Any way, I'm so sorry for not writing back soon. I have to study and also do my assignments. This school year is some kind of hard. I'm a Junior. Next year I'll be graduated from High school.

Well, I'm so glad that you find your job. God bless you. How's your mom, give hi to her from me okay. also your father and your brother. also my best regard.

I hope that you will come to Pohnpei again. If you plan to come back for a visit, write to me okay and tell me when so I will tell my parents and we can go to the airport and pick you up. You can come and stay with us. We will go swimming at the river and also go fishing on the reef. My father loves fishing. This is his Habbit.

Hope to hear from you soon. Bye bye. You were like a father to me.

God Be with you.

JAN-8 1990   Love,

A Former Girl Student on Pohnpei

P.O. BOX 541
Kolonia Pohnpei FSMA 96941
Feb/25/87

Dear Mr. Burkett

Helo! How are you because Frank and all of us are very well. Frank is a good man Dont worry about him because all people are very kind to him. I am very proud of him because he is a good English teacher he also a good basketball coach. Frank told us that you are a very kind man. On Febuary 20. We play against the sekere team they beat us because this is our First year to play basket ball but the sekere team play every year they practice every day for an hour. I am in 8th arad & I play with the Nett A team. Frank coaches 6th grade to 8th grade. We did not practice everyday because he practice oneteam each day after school for an hour. On Febuary, 19 We are very happy because two of our class mates won the SA contest they took their certificate that day. One of them is Mario and one is Sinterson. On Febuary, 21 We took the Pats and Xavier high school test. God will with you where ever you go. I will stop here because I will write my journel that Frank told me to write bye bye

Truely Your

Bradley Rosario

Dear Frank,

Hellow Frank, how are you today.
Thank you for the pictures you send
us. The pictures were very very good.
They were good because if I forget
you I can see the picture and Remember
you.

Frank is a good man because he
teaches me new words and he alway
come on timed like the new words he
teaches us because its make me know
how to speak in english.

Me and Frank alway go to Kolonia
and he buy lit some ice-creams, cokes,
and he took the camera and make some
pictures. Frank was very kind to me. I
like him. I want to go with him in Halampanu.
I don't want him to go away from me.
When I saw his pictures I always
cry. I'm not tell him because I think
I cant go with him

                    your Firiend
                    Wetiner Hairens
                    I'll try to go with
                         you

Dear Parents

First of all I would thanks to our heavenly father for letting me to meet in this letter. I am very excited when frank went to my school and teached me oral english. I am very delighted because he was realy frank. When was started giving us oral I was very happy because I learn how pronaunce some words. And I also knew the meaning of the words. frank is a polite teacher. He was the first teacher who gave me christmas gift. I am very appreciats when he gave me the christmas gift. I was proud of the gift he gave me. frank's issid good man, he teaches me the word I can not pronaunce And he also teac me playing basket ball. I Contented all the thing frank gave me. because if he not came me nett se maybe I could learn oral but it would not very clear for me.

truly yours
Welsin Sanlos

P.O BOX 63
kolonia pohnpei fsm
96941

SERiyNA IFam
P. o. Box 975
KoloniA Pohnpe

Dear Frank Burkett
     We have a good time to write you a letter. How are you
are you fine, me I am realy better. I am Serlyna Ifanlik
we are realy happy for you because you are a good person
you are very cleaver and you are realy smart too. we are
realy happy for you because you always teaching us an
oral English. you do not say something that will hurt us
and you don't make us sad. you want us to be happy.
Why are you leaving from us? If you reach on your land
I want you to write another one letter for me. please
do what did I said. you are a good Coach when you
give our class-mate boys practice for basket ball. please
tell your mom, your sister, and your brother about what
did I write for you Frank! why will you do not
come back again Frank? Frank you know what I want
you If you reach on your Island I want you to
write me a letter and send me a pictures of you, your
brother, your mom, and your sister. Frank please tell
your mom, your brother, and your sister to with you
and send me their letter and pictures of them. Fran
If I have a good time I will write a letter and send
it for you. please Remember me Frank do not forge
me. I will Remember you too. I will not forget you.
I will always write you a letter Frank. Please do not
laugh for my writing because I don't understand spea
in oral English. I know but only a little. Thank
Frank, your mom, your sister and your brother.

          Please Remember my Address
          Welcome to Ponape. bye! bye.
Sorry. my Address is 975
          I love Alabama
               Thank you Frank and your fa

Mark A. Ugohn
P.O. box 620
Kolonia, pohnpei
#96941

Dear Frank

Hellow mr. Buskell how are you, are you fine or not because im very fine. I really miss you frank There is not going here. What about in alabama? I really miss you about teaching me oral English, basket ball and lifting weight. I think I can speak English just a little. frank, I want you to do something for me. Can you send me wrestling books because I like to read them. Remeber the one that you gave me, I really like it. I like the way Jimmy snuka, Hulk Hogan and Ricky Steamboat wrestl. and also send me pictures of Your Parents, and you and your team. My dad told my he likes me to go do SDA with I said okay! so that me and my sister can go to school together. frank, it you want me to send you some letters and pictures, I can send them do you frank. when can you come back to Pohnpei because all of us are really miss you. frank some day it will writing to you. frank can I ask you a question? when can you marri? In what year? frank I had one sister and two brothers. please write me back a letter. by! by! my friend.

From: your friend
Mark anthony Buyoh

Mark A. Buyoh
P.O. box 620
Kolonia, Pohnpei
96911

Frank, one thing left
send me your birthday
month. and God may
be always with you.

Carmela Parapart
P.O.Box 717
Kolonia, Pohnpei
F.S.M '96

Dear Frank,

Hi, how are you? Hope your in a good health than you still stay on Pohnpei. Do you like Pohnpei? I think so.

Well, I thank you and also your parents the way you do to me and my classmates. I's appreciate that. Your a good Oral english teacher. I learn new words and so my classmates. I did not nervous and shy after I stand up infront of the class and speak english. Thank you very much. I like to read papers and books to read. I'm glad you bring some to me and the others to read and so the wrestling books. I like to watch the wrestling in TV. Thanks for the way you shak my hand before the Pics Entrance Tea Test. It makes me feel happy and not nervous. Thank you for everything you do to me and my classmates, and I'm glad you come to NETT. Well, see you some days. Bye, Bye. May God Bless you and your family.

a kiss
your parents
for me, ok.

Your student,
Carmela Parapart

P.O. Box 1415
Kolonia Pohnpei
C.C.I 96941

Dear family,

Before going on I would like to say "Hellow!" How are you. I hope you are as fine as me and Frank. I wold like to tell you that Frank was a teacher in nett school. He teaches some things. He teaches oral english and he also coaches basketball.

I'm realy happy with Frank. Frank was my best friend of all. I knew He loves me. He always talk to me. Frank was a very good man because he gave some gifts to our classmates. I love Frank because He was trying to help us in oral english. Please family Dont be worry about frank because I knew Frank was realy happy on pohnpei. Thank You family. Bye, Bye

Truly Yours,
PRIDOLINO Bergen

Dear Mrs. Burkett,

Before I'll start this letter, I would like to thank to our lord cause he's the one whose saving our own life. I would like to say "Hello" to you, also your family.

My name is Mary Johnson and I live in pohnpei. Your son Frank, Teaches me oral English one period a day, He coaches basketball play. He is really nice guy cause he is kind. He wants my class mates and I, to be nice, and he wants us to be kind, and also he wants us to learn more words from oral English.

I thinks that you are all fine and I want to tell you that He is fine. He wants to learn ponapean words. Maybe he can learn more ponapean customs. I think you are in a good health. and also Franks is doing ok. I might say good bye to you cause I'm really out of words to say.

Bye, Bye May god bless you in. this New year or in all the time.

P. O. Box 1553

Love,
Mary John

P.O Box 184
kolonia Pohnpei
eastern caroline
island 96741

Name: Wayne Mendiola Jr.

Dear Frank;

   How are you. I am very proud of you. You are so kind and good. I'm glad when you came to our school, Because you are good. you are kind. Thank you for teaching us oral English. I had learned many new ideas and words. You always come and teach us.

   Thank you for buying me and Arsenio some cakes and ice cream. Did you remember that. You are very good. You always tell us good job, I am am proud of you, and you always bring some pictures for us.

   You are a good basketball coach. I want you to coach us again for the next season. Thank you for a realy big practice you to for us in basketball. I learn a lot of things in basketball. You always shook our hands when we won the basketball play. I realy enjoy the basketball. If we work a little harder this time, we will be the champion for the next season.

   You are polite, you always tell us I am proud of you. you often talk to us. you always shake our hands. I realy love you. If you go to Alabama, please write me back; and Here is my address at the top of my paper. I want you to come back if you go to albama.

                        Sincerly;
                        your friend;
                        Wayne Mendiola

Rickner Nakasone
P.O. Box 1622
Kolonia Pohnpei 191
E.ci

Dear Frank Burrket

Dear Frank Burrket my name Ps Rickner Nakasone, I was born Pn September 9 1973. Frank Ps my teacher and he Ps also my friend, he has done somethi good for me, He teaches me oral englishand I'm learn some words, he coach basketball and he get 4 team and they win 22 times and lose 9 times, Nett A lose 3 times and Nett B lose 5 times. Pn December 26 1986 they give Frank some gift and he gave all my classmate and me a blak of cake and they eats it. he toke a video to th principals house and they see there. he gave me a new shirt and he toke some news papers and he put Pn th glass room. If someone lPkes to read books he can toke only 1 and 2 and read Pt. One day they cross the Pslar of Pohnpei and played basketball with the other team Pn Palikir and all Frank's team were wPn, when they came bac I went home at 7:45 P.m my mother and Father were h ppy because they new they were wPn and none of Ps te lose. one day Nett B vs SDa and Nett B lose and Nett A vs Sekere B and Nett A lose they were so angry because they lose the game and they want to Fight. They make Frank so sad and he said that he didn't Coach them agaPn because they made him Fight and he didn't Co ach them agaPn. when they played basketball one of the teacher were their Coach but he didn't Know how to Coac basketball because he Ps not a player Im glad you topohnp agaPn Frank. Frank I will remember you. when I'm go to college I tried to write you another letter Frank.

Kennally David
P.O. Box 856
#96941

Dear: Frank

Frank I'm so lonesome because I can't see in ponpei. Frank when you went in Albana I'm so Anger because you can't take me in Hospital. Frank you reumember when you take me in hospital? Frank I remember you when you take me in Hospital. Frank you are a good man. Frank when you live in Europe you teach me oral english and basketball. I'm so happy because I knew how to speak english and I knew how to pass the ball. Frank pleased reuember me when you happy when I happy I _____ reuember you. Frank when you Europe you live in ponpei? Frank I reuember you when you live in ponpei when you live in ponpei my legs are numb you gave me a medicine my legs are not numb. You are a good man, Frank what the work you do in Albana. Pleased asked me. One day I walking on the road I'm so lonesome because I don't joint you on the road when I don't joint you I'm so sad because I like to see you how. Frank pleased when you reuember me pleased write me you letters. Because I like to read you letters. Frank I like to read wresting book can you bring me one. Frank I like so read super fly and road warriers. Frank I think you can sent me one.

Good Luck my
Friend: Your Friend

Kennally David!

Kennally David
P.O. Box 856
Kolonia ponzpe
#96941

P.O Box 441   Kolonia, Pohnpe 444 96941

Dear Peace corp Frank Burkett
My name is Higinia Selgohr. I'm one of your
student in the 8th Grade B. I hope that you still
remember me. I remember the wrestling book you
gave me and I realy like it. Sometimes in the
morning I came in the classrome and read the magazines
and newspapers you gave us. When I reach a new word
you gave us I always remember you. Doctor Frank
thank you for cure my brote hands. You are realy the
best Oral English teacher. You gave us some new
words that we never reach before. You help us to correct
our Grammers and spellings. I realy Glad and I realy
want you to come back in Nett. I am waiting for you to
come back to Pohnpei. I love you Frank.
This boy has scares so bad he couldn't even hold
a pencil.

FRANK, My mother & all my brothers
and sisters were all Thanked you very, very
much for those dozens. They told me to
come and tell you that there isn't any
GRAEF things to pay for, but God blessings

This boys Father was   THANK You very much
Dying. I Gave him a Dozen
eggs. He said that I was   Bergen
the First white man who
ever did anything for him.

name: Arserio. C. Wilson
Address = P.O. Box 69 Pohnp.
Dear Frank. State 96941

Hi!! How are you now? I want to
tell you, thank you for the New words you
teach for me. They are very important because I
Learn somers new words. One day if you come
back I can speak you well. The words that I
know before your come are not high words. Today
you teach me some high words. This make
me feel good. I am very proud of you.
If you not come, Maybe I will not happy.
You make me happy. You teach me how to
play basketball. You give me a shirt. You
Some times you bought so video cassetes and I see
with you. You bought me some ice cream.
You let me to see your wrestling books. You
is the best friend I have. If we lost a
Game, you not angry. You always come to
teach us except when you have a work shop.

P.O. Box 874
Kolonia Pohnpei
F S M #96941
Dec. 18-1986,

Dear Mr. Burcett,

      Hello!! Mr. Burcett, first of all I would like to thank for our heavenly father for giving us a good time task frealy in this poor letter. How are you. I think that you are realy fine as I am. I thought that your family and you were very anticipated for your son to go back, but you son were very happy that the reason why didn't he go back. I loved your son very much.

      Frank is a brilliant and kind man. My classmates and I were very happy with Frank because he coach us basketball and teach us Oral English one period a day. An Frank also give some of us a christmas percent. He gave them watch, shirts and some other good things. We were very delighted because We learned so much in basketball and learned how to make reports in oral english. And we have played our first game and won. Frank and us were very excited when we won the game. This will be a short letter because I am so tired. So please write back this poir letter as soon as possible.

                Farthfuly yours,

                Kastin Rodriguez

>From: <shincine21@hotmail.com>>To: billyjack41@hotmail.com>Subject: Re: the
original record
>Date: Tue, 05 Aug 2003 07:50:46 +0000
>>the original record   *Greenville Advocate, Greenville-AL*
>>By Angie Long (Frank Burkett Story) "Making a 'World' a Difference" *36037*
Or "a   *— 3 more stories done on me*
>World of difference" (Part one of two) " Teacher shares our language *including a*
and   *trip to china.*
>local culture with foreign students"
>>Life used to seem pretty predictable for country boy Frank Burkett. As
a
>rural teen growing up in the '60 and '70 Burkett put in long hours
hauling
>hay and harvesting fields of vegetables in southwestern Butler County.
>At the ends of those back- breaking, dusty, humid days, the tired
young
>man would return to the modest home he shared with parents Edward and
>Louise Burkett.
>His dreams at night seemed to beckon him----to what, he wasn't susre.
Maybe
>they were saying that something more might be out there for him,
something
>different. For Burkett, that "something" began in Greenville at the
old
>Stabler hospital.
>"Dr. Paul Stabler gave me my first 'real' job working in X-ray at the
>[Stabler] hospital in the mid-70s.
>He was so kind and helpful to me, a great man and a great teacher,
>Dealing with this new and exhilarating feeling of self-confidence,
Burkett
>decided to start night school at LBW. He went on to study social
science at
>Troy State University.
>It took him seven years to earn his degree as he worked full-time to
pay
>his way while attending classes part -time. As the years passed he
never
>gave up on his dreams of faraway places and new challenges.
>"I would watch TV and see all these places around the world. I knew if
>given the chance I would go, meet new people, learn new customs,"
explainx
>Burkett, adding,"[I wanted] to make the world a better place to live
in...
>I wanted to make a difference."
>Burkett began making a difference right here in Alabama. In 1983, he
was
>selected as the Montgomery County Youth Volunteer of the Year for his
>efforts to help trcubled local youth.
>By 1986, Burkett had joined the Peace Corps, becoming a teacher in
>Micronesia, part of a chain of over 1,200 islands near Guam. At first,
the
>rural area to which he was assigned seemed familiar, but it turened

out to
>have some unusual local customs.
>" The women were topless- that 'turned your head' for about two weeks until
>you got used to it. I knew I wasn't in Alabama [anymore]." Burkett remarks
>sheepishly.
>He was later shocked to learned from the school's headmaster that the male
>students thought Burkett didn't like them. It was the native custom among
>men, the headmaster explained, to show physical affection----hugging.
>walking arm in arm----toward their friends and acquaintances. Burkett
>learned there was no sexual intent in their behavior; the villagers simply
>had no concept of the Western idea of respecting someone else's "space".
>Burkett also discovered women were not allowed a real voice in the
>Micronesian community. Females were expected to walk 10 feet behind any
>male, unless they were married to him. (then, it was acceptable to walk
>side by side)
>Burkett admits his surprise over his tremendous popularity with American
>Peace Corps women when he first arrived in Micronesia. Turns out, he says,
>" I was the biggest guy and [became]known for having a lot of wives." The
>female Peace Corps workers knew the local men would not 'hit on' them when
>they walked the streets in the presence of the big, burly American, Frank
>Burkett.
>>Burkett asjusted to his new home and worked at making that positive
>difference. During his two years in Micronesia he established a basketball
>league for 900 middle school boys.
>The students and their 20 coaches learned all about dribbling, free throws
>and guarding the ball from Burkett----and a supply of videotapes. "It was
>hard...they[the Micronesians] had never seen a game of basketball on TV,"
>Burkett admits.
>From Micronesia, Burkett journeyed to Seoul Korea in 1988 to teach English
>and by 1990 he was teaching the language in Al-Jubail, Saudi Arabia. Lottle
>did he know at the time Saddam Hussein was planning to invade neighboring
>Kuwait, only an hour's drive away.

>Burkett quickly found himself doing more than teaching language there in
>Saudi Arabia. He and other American citizens would travel to the border
>each weekend to deliver cases of ice-cold soft drinks in coolers and
>supplies of home-cooked meals (including Burkett's trademark crispy fried
>chicken)to the hot, hungry and thirsty American troops stationed there.
>Burkett also snapped photo of over 100 homesick soldiers, had the film
>developed and sent the precious photos back for them to their families in
>their families in the states.
>Most of us are familiar with the televised Christmas greeting from troops
>stationed overseas. Burkett assisted in making some of those tapes while
>living in Al-Jubail. Looking back on his Saudi experience, Burkett says he
>was probably "crazy" to stay there with scud missile going over five times
>a night. Yet, he doesn't regret it, saying, " I believed I was helping and
>doing a lot of good, so I stayed."
>He admits the brutal and unforgiving nature of Saudi culture may have been
>almost tougher to deal with than the ever-present threat of bombs, saying,
>" Their laws require deep vengeance—yot steal and get caught, your hand is
>cut off, even if it's your first offense. I saw several guys walking around
>with only one hand.
>"there were no womwn in my classes there. You weren't supposed to look at
>them or apeak to them in public. If they were seen out with a man it had
>better be a relative.
>There was a good chance if you are an unfaithful woman and get caught you
>would be stoned to death for adultery just like in the Old
>Testament...basically, dogs get more respect than women because wives are
>just property to them."
>Burkett recalls a groups of clergy at his school who would take every issue
>of magazines showing so much as a bare arm or leg. Any bare female flesh
>was an obscenity in their culture.
>Multiple marriages, however, were perfectly acceptable. One of Burkett's
>Saudi students, a 21- year-old, had 223 brother and sisters and three

By Angie Long

Tales from the Far East"

Butler County native experiences China first-hand

(Frank Burkett travel story)

Georgiana native Frank Burkett has had many fascinating experiences in his lifetime. He taught dozens of Micronesian students the fine art of a sport they'd never seen before-- basketball. He took risks to deliver his own crispy homemade fried chicken and plenty of ice cold Cokes to hungry American troops in Saudi Arabia during the Gulf War.

The former Peace Corps volunteer and veteran teacher has shared home-cooked meals with students in need, given away clothing and, at times, provided a safe haven for a young person cast out of home.   Burkett considers it all 'in the line of duty' as a concerned citizen of the world.

For the past ten years, Burkett has been an English teacher in Korea and will soon begin his third year as an instructor at Korea's Pyong-Taek University. This January Burkett had "the opportunity of a lifetime"-- a week-long visit to the People's Republic of China. All expenses were covered for this "fantastic experience" by Pyong-Taek.

Burkett and other university staff visited their 'sister' school, Qufu Teacher's University in China's Shandong Province. They journeyed to sights both ancient (Confucius' burial place) and modern (a high-tech brewery that has been visited by numerous international heads of state, including George Bush).

"China is a beautiful country, truly a mixture of the old and the new. You see both big cities with modern buildings and tiny country villages with simple huts where life hasn't changed much since the time of Genghis Khan," notes Burkett.

Even though China is Communist, capitalism and Western culture seem to be making strong inroads into this vast country. The 'Golden Arches' dot the landscape.

Burkett taps a photo of himself standing along side the Chinese 'version' of Colonel Sanders. "Like the Chinese people, he seemed a little smaller than his American counterpart," Burkett remarks with a grin.

Large discount stores, part of a French chain similar to Wal-Mart, can be found in the cities. And while there are no movie 'megaplexes', karaoke rooms or pool halls, there are bowling alleys and Internet 'chat rooms' (open 24 hours a day, seven days a week) in today's China. Vast farm fields-necessary to feed one of the world's most populous nations-- can be seen throughout the Chinese countryside.

"I saw great poverty and great wealth, even though such extremes don't officially exist in a Communist country. There are not supposed to be any beggars, but I encountered a number of people on the streets who were doing just that," says Burkett.

Burkett found the Chinese people "extremely nice and friendly...I worried at first that they might react negatively to me as an American, but that was not at all the case. They were wonderful, full of questions for me. I think I was really treated better than the Koreans," he notes.

He was careful to respect local customs when taking photographs to document his trip. "Many people in other parts of the world believe that having their photo taken will steal their spirit, so I was always careful to ask permission. Not everyone agreed to be photographed but many people were nice enough to let me snap their picture," he says.

Browsing through Burkett's photo album, you'll find shots of eye-catching wooden horse-drawn 'taxis' with bright painted designs on the sides. There are bicyclists everywhere. Smiling street vendors sell popular Chinese snacks to passers-by.

"On the streets of China you can find baked sweet potatoes, boiled peanuts, bunches of radishes and something that looks like a stack of meatballs on a stick-I never was completely sure what that was," Burkett says.

Burkett largely enjoyed his foray into Chinese cuisine. "If you like good southern cooking, you will love traditional Chinese food-it's very similar," he notes. He even discovered the Chinese have a sweet form of that favorite southern staple, grits. He did take exception to one popular Asian dish, stewed chicken served with its head intact on the plate ("I just don't like having my food looking back at me.").

Burkett had the opportunity to visit the 2,500-year-old grave site of Confucius and his descendants and found himself favorably impressed by the teachings of this famed Chinese philosopher.

"Some of what he [Confucius] said reminded me of the teachings of Christ...and actually the religion goes back even further [than Christianity]. What's amazing to me is how they've traced his genealogy down through all the years. He has over four million descendants around the world today, including a direct tie to a professor in Taiwan," Burkett says.

His return trip to Korea didn't go as smoothly as his visit to China. Fog kept the airport completely shut down so the group had to travel for six hours to the coast to take a ship back home. Quarters on board were certainly 'close'.

"There were fifteen of us sleeping in one room together, very crowded...and the seas were rough. You can't sleep too well in a ship constantly pitching back and forth and sideways. All I could think of was the Titanic. It took 18 hours for us to reach land and I sure was glad to put my feet on dry land...still, I was so glad I got to go. It was a dream come true," Burkett notes.

Burkett has enjoyed the chance to visit with friends 'back home' and the opportunity to see his mother Louise Burkett, a resident of Georgiana Nursing Home. (He's also pretty happy to get some "real beef" burgers and say a temporary 'goodbye' to the ever-present rice dishes of Asia.)

Still, he admits he's looking forward to his return to the place he now considers home, South Korea, where he will soon begin a new academic year at Pyong-Taek.

He recently received the title of professor, a new office and computer, a pay raise and (perhaps most important) a promise that his class sizes will decrease in the coming school year ("Reading 500 papers at a time-and I do read them all-will wear you out.").

He'll be teaching classes in English and a new course on research. As in years past, Burkett will use back issues of "The Greenville Advocate" as an important tool to teach the language and share American culture and customs with his students.

He'd love to have some Butler County students become pen pals with his Pyong-Taek students and encourages interested educators to contact him at his e-mail address: outsidecastle16@hotmail.com.

"I really do love my students. In many ways they are like family to me. Whatever I can do to help them, sharing my time, knowledge, possessions–even my home-- I am glad to do it.

" I know there's a lot of bad things going on in the world that I can't do a thing about. But I've discovered ways I can make a positive difference...including sharing my life experiences with others," Burkett notes.

With a gracious smile, the tall, mustachioed American makes a slight bow joined with a single firm shake of the hand ("That's a handshake, Korean-style) before heading off to enjoy the rest of his visit.

Doubtless this homegrown goodwill ambassador will take back many tales of life in the U.S.A–along with a suitcase "crammed with newspapers" from the Camellia City - to his curious Korean students.

8

HEALTH CARE, SICKNESS, AND I'M THE DOCTOR

First of all I want to say that I'm not a doctor, I worked three years in a hospital and I have been certified in CPR, Red Cross First Aid, have a lot of knowledge in health care, but I'm not a doctor. But any doctor is better than no doctor over there. I'll tell you about some of the things that I ran across over there. The first one that I want to talk about is named Higino. Higino was on my basketball team and I'd never noticed him, I knew of him, but with so many boys, I could never take time to talk to that many. One of the boys came up to me one day and said, "Frank, would you please help Higino?" I asked what do you mean? He said, "He's got sores so bad that he hurts." So I looked and on his hands there were sores so bad that he couldn't even hold a pencil in school and could hardly walk because they were so bad. It mostly had to do with a little insect called scaibes malnutrition and personal hygiene. I felt so sorry for him and was moved by compassion so. He was a cute little guy, rosy red skin all over. You could see the Japanese from his grandfather's line, all the way down. So I carried him to where my room was and I said let me see your sores. He had them all over his body and I said oh, boy, I've got a lot of work cut out here, so I put peroxide and first of all had to bathe him all over, literally with soap and water. I guess I spent an hour or two with him, three or four times before I was able to cure him.

Higino passed his high school test that he was supposed to take for the school and to this day he still calls me Dr. Burkett. He wrote me a letter not long ago and told me that he adopted me as part of his family and when I come back I could stay with them and I had a place to lay down in his house. They give me entitlement to food or anything else with any of his relatives on the Island. That was Higino.

The next one that I want to talk about is Rivally. He was a tall boy, but he was not from the Island, he was from Truk. Being from Truk he was considered an outcast. He was living with his brother and his current home wasn't anything, really. He was left to raise himself and I mean that Literally in terms of raising himself. Rivally was left out of any kind of party or anything the other boys went to, because he was from Truk. It was the custom in Nett, the municipality that I lived in that the people would go beat up anybody from Truk that came along, though they didn't beat Rivally up. He was just not treated right.

I noticed that he never could run. so, I started talking to him one day and he had real shortness of breathe and I thought he might have TB. I went with him to the doctor, we stayed there I guess, two or three hours. I'll talk more about the doctors and the hospital later on. Finally we got to see a doctor. The doctor came in and looked at him and started treating him. I knew that if Rivally had TB, then I also had TB, so that was one of the worries on my part. The doctor was one of the few American doctors there. For a doctor or for anybody, she was one of the cutest girls you could ever look at, though she must have been in her thirties to have gotten her MD degree. She was really treated bad in the hospital because she was American. Americans are not treated well working at the hospital. Doctors tend to be spoiled here in America but when they get there all of a sudden they're in the real world. They have to do their own thing, there's nobody to run errands for them and things like that. She treated ham and gave him some antibiotics and within seven days Rivally was up running and playing and having the best time. After that I said well, we'll fix you up a little more. I asked him if he had ever been to the dentist and he hadn't. So for about the next three weeks in a row, Rivally and I went to the dentist to have his teeth cleaned and then to put fillings in his teeth. Otherwise, he just simply would never have done it. It wasn't TB and we got his teeth fixed and he came out real good things went well for him. He passed the test for the only public high school on the Island. He didn't really pass it. He came in 58 or 59 before passing but they didn't have that many to reach the top levels so they chose him as one to go. I was real happy about that. Today he's in the public school. I don't think his grades are doing too well. He wrote me at Christmas time and wanted $50.00 and I didn't have $50.00 to send him, and I really wouldn't have because he would probably have ended up buying liquor and whiskey with it. I didn't want him to do that.

The next one I want to talk about is Jordan. Jordan. You could look at him and see the Spanish descent in him. His last name is Gallen. but they pronounce it CAllen. Jordan is one of the smartest fourteen year olds I've ever met, anywhere. He can just pick up a word of English or anything and go with it like no one I've ever seen. Jordan starts out, how I managed to get in touch with this guy, I had the boys running out in the schoolyard one day, and I noticed that Jordan was getting into a bad shape. I stopped him and set him down. Remember, I don't have the luxury of having a doctor, or an ambulance within walking distance, much less driving distance of me. So I am it. So I sit him down and the principal carries him in and lays him down behind her desk and I loosen his clothes, where he can breathe. His eyes are dilated and his running about one hundred and forty beats a minute. He's real cold and sweaty feeling. It scares me, I'm thinking he's going to have a heart attack or something. I don't know. It was eleven o'clock. About two o'clock, I still stayed with him and the teachers and all the other Pohnpeins thought it was very unusual that I, an American, would be caring about a Pohnpein. But after a while, the principal came in, and I asked her if O could walk with Jordan down to the hospital. She said, "Yes, that'll be fine." So, we went down to see this same doctor, whom I have mentioned before and this go around she sort of scolded me a little bit. The reason she did is because if something came up with one of my students that I didn't have an answer to I went to her and she thought I might be over reacting. But she was a specialist and I wasn't and I wasn't going to take the chance. So she scolded me real good but that's all right. She must have had a bad day. It took us about two hours to see her at the hospital and she listened to his heart and said it could be a heart murmur, she wasn't sure. So she said, "I'll run EKG, an x-ray, and do some lab work." When I say all these things, it's not exactly the professional health care that you are looking for, that we have here in America. So on the way out, Maria happened to be there, the principal, getting her teeth filled. A real status symbol on the Island to have a gold tooth. So, she was getting several gold teeth put in. She said "I'll carry Jordan home, and I'll carry you home." Which, my walk was about 40 minutes away, Jordan was even a much longer ride. My principal said that her husband had went to this doctor the week before and she was a bad doctor, and these kinds of things. I didn't think she was bad because I'll tell you later on in my writings why she was not a bad doctor. She asked, "What the doctor say?" I said she said that Jordan couldn't play for the week until we found out the results of his tests. Our principal said, "I'm not too worried about that, you can go ahead and play him now if you want to." I said, "No ma'am, I can't do that. I'm sorry." She said, "I said you could." I said, "No, we can't." I told her that if Jordan played on the ball team that I was coaching and I knew that he wasn't supposed to then I wouldn't coach it anymore. I had to say that and I meant that too! A week went by and Jordan was mad as he could be because I hadn't let him play basketball. Jordan was real quiet, he wouldn't say anything to me, he was mad at me because I wouldn't let him play, but his health was more important than a basketball game. So, he told me that his mother was coming. So, I said

"Okay, you and I have an appointment so we will go see the doctor and Maria can tell your mother where we are." So we walked down by a little store and I said, "Jordan, do you want a drink?" He said no, but anyway I bought him one. We got there, his mother came later on, the doctor had checked him out and found out that he was okay and didn't really know what the cause was, maybe he had the flu or something. He had a good bill of health. She said he could play ball again. I was so happy about that. On the way back, his mother actually thanked me, which was unusual, for standing by Jordan the way I did. I felt good about that and when I left he even waved good-bye to me. That's about as much thank you as I guess I could get from a fourteen year old. Jordan is at the college prep school at Truk now and I think he is doing real good. He's a brilliant young man and I look for him to be a leader that Micronesia really needs.

KENNLEY—The next young guy that I want to talk about is Kennley. Kennley is eighteen or nineteen in the eighth grade, I guess his parents kept him out of school, I don't really know. Kennley never talked to me, he kept his distance from September until January. When I was grading his journal I read in his journal that he had a numbness in his legs and he couldn't get up in the mornings. He had no feeling in his legs so I got real concerned and I talked to him about it. He told me that it was true. I said, "Let's go see the doctor." He said, "Okay." His English wasn't good enough for him to explain to the doctor and I said, "Well, write it down in Pohnpein, how you feel and I'll have the teacher, my co-worker here, translate it for me, so that I can tell the doctor how you are feeling." He said, "Okay." Before we made the appointment to go to the doctor, it was about three weeks before I could get free a day to go to the doctor, because I was tied up every solid day. I would buy Ben-Gay sports cream and before every basketball game I would put it on his back and his legs, so that he could play. Pretty soon after got around that it was a miracle drug all the other players wanted it, standing in line to have it rubbed into the back and legs, Ben-Gay, because they'd heard about it. I walked with him, down to the hospital and the doctor checked it out. It was a pulled muscle and Kennley got along okay. He wrote in his journal before I left that when I would leave Pohnpei he would have a big cry, and how he would miss me and who would be there to carry him to the doctor when he needed to go. Different things like that, and it really made me feel good. I won a friend in Kennley.

JUNIOR—Junior was a tall boy, he had a background like you wouldn't believe, he was the principal's son. Junior has Pohnpein, Trukese, German, and maybe Spanish in his background, I'm not sure. Anyway, he was a tall boy, had beautiful eyes, his skin was dark, his hair was curly. He was as smart as he could be and I used to get tickled watching Junior. His responsibility every day was to feed the pigs. He's like any other fourteen year old, he didn't like to do chores. It was December before Junior would come up and talk to me. It took months for some of my students to ever say anything to me. At Christmas time some of my students gave me presents and Junior came at a later date and gave me a sculpture of a dolphin. It was real pretty. Getting back to Junior's health care, he came by to visit me one night and I asked, "Junior, what's wrong with your toe?" He was limping and I looked at it. He had been cutting grass with a machete and had just cut the middle down it and parted it. I said, "Oh, Junior this looks bad, you've got to take care of it." He wouldn't go to the doctor, so I said I'll do my best. So, I put peroxide on it and cleaned it out good, put antibiotic cream on it and then made a butterfly stitch. After I made butterfly stitch, and put that on there, I did that about four times over a two week period, and his toe got along okay. Junior is now in the college prep school on Truk doing real good, his father wants him to be a lawyer because his father is a state representative. Junior wants to be a priest. Junior wrote to me the other day and told me that when we meet again, one day, he will carry me to the nicest and fanciest restaurant in the world. So I look forward to that trip one day.

HOSPITAL, PEACE CORPS AND OTHER THINGS
PEACE CORPS

The Peace Corps Medical Staff did an excellent job in taking care of us as far as our medical kits and check-ups went. Every three months they would give us a GG shot, or gamma gobulin, which is supposed to stop hepatitis. It seemed like every time I went into the Peace Corps office someone was telling me to drop my pants. GG shots never come easy. They'd go into the hip and its a pretty hard shot to take. They made your right leg stand up. The other thing that I did as for as my health care is every time I would get water (the gamma gobulin shot was supposed to have been sixty percent success rate in preventing hepatitis, which is real bad on the Island) so the rest of the time I would use iodine tablets to put in my water. That kept me from getting hepatitis. On Pohnpei you can come down with a sickness more than any place you've ever seen in your life. You can have diarrhea so fast, you can run a 102 or 103 degree temperature, and be four days that way. It's just unbelievable how that can happen. But it did.

MY SICKNESS

It started out on the weekend, my family went off on a trip somewhere, left me there with one of the teenagers to do my cooking for me. I got real sick and I spent the whole weekend in my room. I was so sick that I couldn't go to the bathroom, so I took a empty water jug and would urinate in it so I wouldn't have to get up. I kept another jug so I could have drinking water so that I wouldn't dehydrate. Monday morning, I knew I was sick and almost passed out, and I said "I've got to get to the doctor some way. So I started out walking, It's over an hours walk to the Peace Corps office, and I didn't have anyone to pick me up. I made It there and when I got there, they rushed me in and laid me down, my blood pressure was 160 over 110, my pulse rate was 115, my temperature, when I got there was 99 degrees, within ten minute, it went to 101. They took me to the hospital, gave me six bottles of IV over an eighteen hour period. My temperature in a few minutes went to 103. All of this within twenty-four period. I had a headache that just about blew my mind off, just blew my head off. Within those twenty-four hours, I lost ten pounds, weighing at one time two forty-eight, down to two thirty-eight, I was eating only soup because that was the only thing that could stay inside me. I had to go to the bathroom ten to twelve times a day. They found pus in my stool specimen. While I'm at the hospital, I get a good initiation into it. It's one giant ward, no private, no semi-private rooms, no hospital gowns. I stayed in my bed in my overalls, when I'd go to the bathroom I would have my IV bottle dragging along beside me, in the bathroom several times I had to do mortal combat with a rat. I was scared he'd get inside my pants and I couldn't do anything about it. I couldn't have much anyway. In the hospital, the floors are full of family members sleeping, because that's their tradition, if someone is in the hospital, the family stays with them. I had laid my billfold up on the bed and this kindly gentleman walked by and told me to please put it away, that someone would steal it from me if they saw it. I was put on a liquid breakfast, liquids all the way around. I guess it was the cook in the kitchen who brought me a gallon of apple juice, and that was my three meals a day—to drink that apple juice. I stayed in my overalls, If we got a chance to take a bath, nurses don't come around to ask you that, the doctor, the American doctor that I told you about, came around and checked on me about every hour, taking my blood pressure, temperature and so on. I was like a dishrag, I couldn't get out of bed, hardly, my temperature was so high. They kept those IVs going into me real fast. I was just like a dishrag, so I never felt any pain. When I finished up my twenty-four hour stay, it was just about as good to go somewhere else. The Peace Corps at that time had a house and I went there and another good Peace Corps volunteer named Dave, who was supposed to go on outer island, stayed there and took good care of me. Otherwise, I don't know how I would have managed. But, sickness can come so fast over there, anything you get, they usually call it food poisoning, because they don't have much other term but most of the food is kept out anyway and you don't know when it has been fixed or what. I got along okay with that, got sick many more times. After seventeen months I had developed what they first called—they said I had a flu virus—after the flu virus was over and I was running a temperature that high. I was so hot that even my bed was hot. It was hotter than when I knew it was 103. I didn't know anything. I was out of it. From there I went to strep throat, then a few week later, before I could get over that, I had what one doctor called pneumonia, when I went back the second time, he called it bronchitis. After seventeen months, I figured my body was telling me something and that's when I decided my tour of duty was through.

9

THINGS IN A DAY THAT MIGHT BE AVERAGE

The biggest thing in my whole day usually was going to my mail box. Remember I said it took one solid hour to walk from my house to where the Peace Corps office was, to get your mail. That was a big event. I was getting reading materials from home. Sometimes it would take twelve or fourteen days for you to get it. My parents would send me wrestling books, to keep up with wrestling, newspaper, any kind of reading material, because we didn't have it. I would be off the road come four o'clock in the afternoon, because of drunks.

PMA—JOE'S FRIED CHICKEN

For my regular days, every Wednesday night I had a group called the PMAs—Pacific Missionary Organization—come pick me up for a Bible study and carry me to another American's house. I really enjoyed that. The PMA people there were very kind and nice to me. One guy had been there for thirty years, Reverend Edward Kelow. Joe, a young guy had a wife named Regina, both of them were from Germany and they had been so good to pick me up that I wanted to do something nice for them. So I went to the little store and bought two chickens—paid five dollars a piece for small chickens. Joe and Regina had never eaten Southern fried chicken. I couldn't get over someone who had never eaten any fried chicken. I cooked it for them and while I cooked, we cooked it on a kerosene stove and they ate it. They ate every bit of that chicken and loved it. I know that when they went back to Germany, they taught some of those Germans how to cook good Southern food. Too bad I didn't have turnip green and crackling bread. That would have surely put them in hog heaven.

SAMSON

Samson, when I first saw him was a young guy, I would say twenty-three or twenty-four. He didn't look any different from anybody else, but I was soon to find out things about him that were really scary. they had said that Samson had been on marijuana since he was a boy and was still on it. This was nine o'clock one Saturday morning I'd just gotten up, I could hear the birds outside my window, singing. How pretty and nice the view was, I could look at the ocean and waves coming in, it was just a beautiful day. All of a sudden I heard this knock at my door, a bang like. I looked out my window and Samson had went into the family's deep freeze—at that time the family had a deep freeze—and was taking out chickens and beating them against the door. Now they were dead chickens but still beating them against the door. He went in and took a five pound bag of rice and threw it out on the yard and one of the men in the family heard what was going on. The mother, my host mother at that time was very frightened. She was back in the corner and I was on my way out to help her because he looked like he was going to do her bodily harm. This other family member came up and slapped him real hard on the head after he did that, he told him to leave. Reluctantly Samson did leave. I didn't know the history of this guy. I said I hope Samson does leave and never comes back. In about a month's time, he was back again. This time it was six o'clock in the morning and all of a sudden the girls in the family had gotten up to cook breakfast. They usually cooked pancakes, real good. They had gotten up and were cooking pancakes and he had been out drinking all night and he came in and he started throwing everything all over the place. Then my host father woke up and came down and Samson jumped on him and the violence was so in the air and at this time one of the family members, his name was Sauce, one of the kindest people you'll ever want to meet, came and stood in my room for my protection so that Samson wouldn't come in and hurt me. They held Samson down and put handcuffs on him, I don't know where they got handcuffs, I found out that that was quite a pattern of his history. They held him down and it was a very violent shaking experience, really fearful for your life. Not so much what he could with you face to face because he was smaller but because he was a coward and he would get you when you least expected it. He could have easily done that with me, where I slept. Anyway the father sent him away. In their culture my host father's grandfather would not let my father send him away for over a month, then he came back and the same thing would happen time and time again. So you see a conflict where the older and the younger generation meet each other. I guess the grandfather thought everyone always picked on

Samson or something and he wanted to stand up for him when in reality Samson would be a very violent mean person who needed to be locked up so that he wouldn't hurt anyone.

COMING HOME AND THE BOY IS

One day I had went to get my mail and come back to my place and I walked in the door and as soon as I walked in the door, one of the teenagers in the family, I guess he was fifteen or sixteen. My host mother at that particular place was thirty-six or thirty-seven. She didn't have a top on which most women over there don't, the breast are for child-rearing only, there's nothing obscene about it. He was down on the floor with her and he was massaging her breast with coconut oil, all up in the top, she was groaning and moaning but that was well accepted as part of their culture and I looked at it and said, "Woo, I am in another world."

USDA FOOD

To show you how fast our government can work, they had a typhoon hit the Island in March. In December the United States government finally got around to sending them relief. In the form of USDA food, they brought it by the tons on the Island. What was so unusual about this is that the Pohnpeins got their first taste of corn, orange juice, Pet milk, homogenized milk. They loved the rice, but my family found out that I loved the orange juice and I needed liquids especially to survive in that hot, humid climate. They would bring me cases of orange juice and leave it my room. One drawback was that when you opened the can you had to drink it all because if you wait, you'll get sick from it, because of the poison. So, I got real tired of having orange juice all the time when you had to drink a whole gallon at one time. The USAD food was really used by the Island people, they really enjoyed it. I saw a lot of people eat it and get a good nutritional meal out of it, which was really good.

RELAXING

I guess that the biggest relaxation I had there was they had a restaurant and hotel on the Island, it was called Palm Terrace. It had an eating place, grocery store and hotel all together in one thing. I would, on a few occasions, rent a room. The room was $32.00, $36.00, somewhere in that area. I'd rent the room and they had three videos in this particular place. I'd rent a room with a video. I never will forget, I'd get John Wayne and the Alamo, Fess Parker in Davy Crockett, king of the Wild Frontier. I had the luxury of having a nice hot bath, and I would take about six baths before I would leave out in the twenty-four period. That was quite a treat, I would buy me a drink and some potato chips and go into my room and it had an air conditioner and I would turn that thing on as high as it would go and enjoy myself. Another treat that I would have is usually twice a week, they had a little restaurant called the Joy. It was like a small town restaurant and it was more catered to the Western people and their foods. I would go in two or three times a week whenever I would walk into town and the waitresses already knew what I wanted, fried chicken, it was all dark meat, pretty hard, nothing like Southern fried but it was very good when you haven't had much to eat like that. They had corn, and green salad, (in their salad they would put Chinese cabbage, cucumbers, seaweed) soup, which was very good. I would order a coke float which was a coke with a scoop of ice cream in the top, a glass of tea, and a glass of water. I knew their water was pretty good, I could drink it and I wouldn't get sick. Also they had one of the luxuries that you like, they had an indoor toilet. Whenever you could go and sit down and relax, it was quite enjoyable.

WATCHING THE VIDEO

This was a past time all over the Island any place that had a video or electricity. Twenty per cent of the Island has electricity, less have video. But in front of the video would be twenty-five to thirty people or more sitting down watching it. They didn't care what was on, they just watched it. I rented a video that was very big, it was Lt. Robinson Crusoe. It was a Walt Disney video. I'd never seen people laugh so much in my life as they did. The could relate to this man on this Island with the coconut trees. They could relate to it real good. They got a real big laugh out of that. What's bad about the video is America has introduced the videos that are extremely violent. I'm not talking about pornography, I could care less about that but in the violent aspects is the way women are belittled, and raped and all. A lot of men on the Island use that as an excuse to treat their women the same as they see on the videos. Because, you remember that if you didn't have knowledge of the newspaper and know what was reality and what wasn't and you see this and you remember your ancestors telling you about how great America was because they ran the Japanese out. If American men treat their women that way on the video then it should be right. That has had a very negative effect on the people on the Island.

CHRISTMAS

I, being a caring person, as I've always looked at myself, one of my stronger traits is my compassion, for the people. The kids on the Island would have one shirts, one watch, and I gave them out at Christmas. Of course the kids were real happy to receive it, they had never received a new shirt in their life. They'd always had hand-me-downs one or two shirts if it was still in good condition. They only had two shirts a year, one for school and one for church. So I did that, but there's a drawback to it. In their culture if there is an older person in the family that likes what you've got and you are the youngest and they want it, they take it. So most of my shirts ended up on the older or the father of the family, which was real hard for me to understand. Anyway, at Christmas time we had a party at the school. The tree was decorated in carbon paper, pretty, real decorated. They didn't have any money to buy Christmas ornaments or anything. So they just stuck a tree up, put the paper on the tree. I was a guest of honor. We had ice cream, which was quite a treat, some of them had never had it. Had a piece of cake and the cake was furnished by an old lady, who lived where my mother lives in Alabama, had sent it to me for Christmas. So I shared it with all the students who were there. They totally loved it, they don't get things like that.

At Christmas time, my students gave me ten present. I was very humble. Most of the students who gave me presents were ones that I didn't give anything to so that meant a lot to me. Their presents might consist of a bar of soap, a pen, pencil, one boys family had a government job and he gave me a real nice shirt. One boy gave me a dollar, it took months for him to get a dollar. One day gave me something that just really humbled me, I opened it up, it was wrapped in a package, real big, as big as your forearm and I said to myself, "What in the world is this?" I looked at at and it was a cucumber. On the Island the greatest gift you can give anybody is food. He gave me the best thing that he could give me. After the party, I took three of the boys, we walked into Kolonia. The reason I took this particular three was the three of them had no father. One of them was Mario, the boy that got beat up over me. We were walking along the road and walking across the river, my mother had sent Mario a wrestling book. Mario was looking at he wrestling book and I jumped him like you are going to scare someone or play someone. At that time the book went up in the air and went downthe river. Mario was so sad and we didn't know how we would get it out. I looked down there and saw a small house and I said, "We'll walk down there and get it." I didn't know if this guy would come out shooting or not. I'd heard that he was real bad on the Island anyway. We went down there and he had some bad dogs. They came out but they didn't bother us. I couldn't speak enough of the language, I tried to tell the man, I figured he understood English a little bit. I told him we had lost a magazine, a book in the river and we wanted to get it out. He was real helpful in getting the book out. I thanked him in their language as well as I could. Walking up the hill, the boys started laughing. I said, "Guys, what are you laughing at?" They said "What that man said." I asked, "What's that?" You told him that your baby fell into the river, and he was wondering why you weren't excited about losing your baby. The boys had a big laugh out of that.

We went into town, for the first time I bought some of the boys cheese. They'd never eaten cheese before. They just chewed and chewed trying to look like they enjoyed it. We went to the Joy, the little restaurant and bought them a coke float, they had a big time, they'd never sat in a chair in their life to eat a meal, have a drink and ice cream. Quite a treat. There was this other little place, a restaurant where you could go. Most of the time if you would bring in a video, they'd let you sit. The boys liked wrestling so we rented a video and watched a wrestling video. The boys had a real good time. It was the first time anybody had ever done anything like that for them. We went back home and the next day was Christmas day, that night, Christmas Eve, I spent that time in my room because I knew the Island would be wild with drunks. Because American companies love to make that money, and it was American beer. I saw some of the young students, none of mine, that were drunk, wobbling in the road. I felt real sorry for them. They were really in bad shape. It's pitiful to see them like that.

EATING PIZZA, ICE CREAM

They had a dance show on the Island, so I invited my little brother to go. After the dance show was over we wanted to eat pizza at this little restaurant. My little brother had never eaten pizza before, so we ordered it. He wasn't too impressed with it, as I wasn't when I first ate it, when I was 25. We always preferred peas and beans. I bought a gallon of ice cream and he ate it. I made him eat till he almost got sick because he was the youngest in the family and unless they didn't want it, he didn't get it. The other volunteer that went with us was running his mouth when he should have kept quiet because earlier in the day I had told him some rather secret thoughts, that a friend would tell another friend. He's sitting there with his big mouth, telling Tony, my little brother, about my thoughts. Tony just looked and I didn't think he really understood the English part of it. But the next day my host mother came and knocked on my door and I said, "Yes, Ma'am?" She said, "Tony was telling me that you are looking for a wife on Pohnpei and I've got a good Pohnpein wife that I can let you have." I said, "Whoa, wait a minute now." I sort of talked myself out of that one, a little bit or tried to.

FEAST

The Feast on the Island is real big as I've already mentioned in Chapter four. I developed quite a love for the food and I knew that you could really eat when you got there, because other times your main meal consisted of rice and maybe a chicken, maybe a turkey tail or something like that. I think we ship all of our turkey tails over there. But at a feast you could get all kinds of good food. My students many times would bring me pineapple, banana, mango, yam and taro. All the time bringing it to my house so that I could eat it. I loved that food, I love to eat anyway. My family a lot of times would have tuna, which was real good, chicken Saints food. Feasts were always good. Then you went to a feast you carried a certain amount of something. I usually didn't have to carry anything because I was a guest. But if some of the family members of someone I knew died, I'd usually send two chickens, which was quite an honored gift.

LOW

One of the lows I had, I had planned a sports banquet. The sports banquet was supposed to be held at the Catholic Mission on a particular Saturday. To tell you about the guy that I'm dealing with here, my father had sent a lot of seeds for the students to plant at school. This guy was an agriculture teacher at school, so I gave him the seeds. Instead of him letting my students plant the seeds, he gave them all away. Which brought him a high status symbol in the village, because he gave some good seeds away. Also all the papers that I had brought my students all during the year, he had his choir group there one day practicing and he just up and gave all my papers away. My papers were meant to go to my students, when school was out. I should have known better, but I didn't. Four times he would sit down and plan a sports banquet with me and he'd agree with me all the way through, and as I've mentioned before, in an earlier chapter, you can't say no to someone on Pohnpei. So even up until the Friday afternoon, we were going to have the sports banquet Saturday, he still told me that we were going to have it. I went and checked and the man hadn't even rented the little place that we were going to use. He had done nothing. So that was one of my real lows, in that time. Another low was in Education Week.

EDUCATION WEEK

What that is, is supposed to be involvement of all the teachers and students. I was never involved in the PTA meetings, or any kind of picnics or anything because I was American. My principal's main goal was, she knew I was an extremely hard worker, she knew I knew what I was doing and we had a common interest in caring about the students. But as a person, she could care less about me, as far as dealing with me or anything in that manner. So Education Week was on all week long, and I wasn't included. I felt I should have been because I'd gotten so close and worked so hard. I was part of the school.

EATING, SLEEPING

One family I stayed with had a small table so I could eat off of and the other I eat off the floor but both places had one thing in common and that was eating alone. I always had rice, cold or hot, sometimes a turkey tail, turkey wing or hot dog. When I finished up eating all the small kids would come and eat what I left. If I ate everything, then they wouldn't get any food. So I always left a lot.

A few times my host father would eat with me. He didn't like cooked fish so he would eat it raw, something I could never get used to. He was very interested in the use of words I used in love and like. He said what is the difference in relation to food. I said I loved chicken but I liked fish. He said he loved fish but didn't like chicken.

My little brother, Tony, 14 years old would cook for me. The first time he cooked chicken. Blood was running out. I knew then that I had to teach him so the first thing was to get him to wash his hands, then to use a knife and cut into the chicken so that it would cook all the way. He got to be a fairly good cook.

One place I stayed at lived an old woman. I don't think she was family but I think she stayed because she had no place else. Anyway she couldn't hear and she would go to bed and turn the radio as loud as it would go. It was next to where I slept and I couldn't. So about 12:00 the only radio station went off the air and I could sleep unless it was a weekend where outside my window was a Sakua Bar "a man's drink on Pohnpei" made from pepper roots, he would or they would sing all night long about the hard troubles of life. I must say I never got much sleep living there. Sing, Sing, all night long. Over and over again they would sing.

TOILET PAPER

I just love doing for other people. The greatest joy in life is the joy of giving but when it comes to toilet paper, I'm a very selfish man.

One night a distant family member asked me if he could borrow some toilet paper. I said sure. Then another asked and another and finally it was all gone.

I can remember when I used an outhouse in Alabama and You always had a good supply of Sears and Roebuck catalogs but in Pohnpei there was no catalogs, only coconut husk and if you ever use that once on your soft behind, you'll never want to use it again. So any place I went I kept a roll of toilet paper in my back pack and only gave it out to very special friends so if I was ever asked about toilet paper, I just lied and said I didn't have any.

BUYING GROCERIES

Peace Crops or the Pohnpein Government gives $50.00 a month for us to live with a host family. My Peace Corps pay was about $300.00 a month and we were supposed to help the family with expenses.

Just about everything is imported from the U.S., Japan or Austria. So when the ship comes in you could get some goodies. I would go grocery shopping and buy for me and the family. Remember at any given time you might have 10 or more family members to eat. You could buy about any kind of can goods like peanut butter, rice but never any grits. Chickens were about $5.00 a piece. Hamburger prices was out of this world. Butter in a tin can from Austria and very little cheese. You could buy turkey tails by the boxes. I had killed a lot of turkeys in my life but we never eat the tails and I know why now, we shipped them all over to Pohnpei. Turkey tails are good to eat but has so much fat on it.

I lived with one family that had a electric stove with an oven. I asked my mother why she never used the oven. She would go outside the door, cut wood and cook over an open fire. She said that she didn't know how to use it and said let me show you. I took a $5.00chicken, open a tin can of butter to melt so that I could put it on the chicken to bake. I turned the oven to 400 degrees and cooked that chicken for 45 minutes. You're talking about something good. It was finger licking good! I said, "thank you Lord."

Next week my family was going to cook me the same kind of chicken but they turned the oven to 500 degrees and cooked it for 1 hour. That chicken was as hard as leather but I ate and I thanked them so for cooking it but you could chew, and chew and it never got soft but I didn't let them know about that. When I finished the kids came to eat and they couldn't even pull it off of the bone so in a few days my host mother asked me to write down on paper how to bake a chicken.

This family had a deep freeze and inside was always tuna. Fresh from the ocean. Tuna was about 4 to 6 feet long and good gosh almighty, it was good. Sometimes I would buy tuna helper and cook using real tuna. The family loved it.

The Pohnpein diet is very bland so one day I was real lucky to buy in the store some lima beans or dried beans. I cooked them and the family being very polite ate them and said it was good. I had forgot that lima beans causes gas on the stomach so after about two hours no family was left in the house.

10

AMERICA SENDS A MESSAGE AND MY OPINION

AMERICA-POHNPEI: COMPARISON

When you travel to Pohnpei and walk the streets there, one of the first things you notice is the stores, little bitty stores, have the sale of whiskey. You can go anywhere you want to and there are stores that have the sale of whiskey, right alongside Coca-Cola. Pepsi, Dr. Pepper, and coconuts. You can look also on every corner where there is beer and whiskey being sold and you'll find a missionary on every corner. Missionaries are Mormon, Jehovah's Witness, Congregationalist, Bahai Faith, and some I've never even heard of trying to convert you to their way of thinking. So, America is sending a message, you have beer and whiskey on one side and a missionary on the other. One will destroy you and the other will save your soul.

STATE DEPARTMENT OFFICIAL TALKS

One day we were lucky enough to have a State Department Official there to talk to us as a group. He said, "Really, Peace Corps is an extension of the State Department, but it's not on paper." We asked what he meant by this. "Peace Corps is a presence, to be known there, that the United States id there." We asked him for further details on that. He said, "An example is, after we invaded Grenada, the first group of people to go in, was the Peace Corps, after the battle had been fought." So, he made that point, that the Peace Corps is just a branch of the State Department, to be visible among the other foreign countries. He also told us of the political struggles that are going on in the South Pacific, the reason the Peace Corps is in Micronesia, is because if the Philippines fall to the communists, the United States will go back to the Republic of Palu, and make a Naval base there, that's the biggest reason. The second reason is because the United States fought so hard for those Islands, that after World War , the United States sort of thought they were their own. That was according to him. He had been around the world, I think he'd been in Moscow, he said wherever you'd see a Peace Corps volunteer, and they had a party or something for the dignitaries, the first place the Peace Corps would go would be to the food, because wherever they lived, they didn't get food like that. So, you could always tell a volunteer by them going to the food first.

ARGUMENT

When you're in a foreign country, sometimes the locals and especially the ones who have been to America and have seen America, will try to get you into arguments about their country and yours, as to which is the better of the two. Some of these arguments are what I'll share with you now. One Pohnpein guy came up to me and asked me what I thought about abortion. You have to realize that when you answer a question. you need to know where this guy came from in an educational background, can he even comprehend that someone has been on the moon, much less talking about abortion, with feelings running as high as they do that issue. Anyway, he made his point really clear. He said that on Pohnpei, every family has between eight to twelve children, that they love all their children, and as long as the family can eat, the children can eat, and as long as the family has the cloths, the kids have cloths. He said, you in America, you call yourselves a Christian nation, yet and still, you kill your children, you kill your babies before they even have a chance to be born, and you still call yourselves a Christian nation.

HOMELESS

A Reverend I was talking to one day had a chance to visit the United States of America, while he was there, he had noticed that in the railway yard, on the streets of the big city where he was that there were people who slept in their same clothes, who slept on the side walks, who had nothing to eat, nothing to wear and nowhere to go. We call them, in America, the homeless. He looked at me and he said, "On Pohnpei, we have no homeless, no one would be without food, no one would be without clothes, no one would be without a family. America puts its own outside in the cold to freeze to death."

NURSING HOMES

Another Pohnpein gentleman asked me about nursing homes. He said, "I come to America and I see that when the old people have finished whit their years in lift that as quickly as you can, you put them in a nursing home and you leave them. "He said, On pohnpei our old people are respected, are looked upon highly in the village and because of their age, whatever they say goes, regardless. We have no nursing homes on Pohnpei, our families take care of them in their own homes."

CHURCHES

When you come to America and look at the largest Protestant denomination in America, it seems like they're trying to build a building to the sky. They have the central air, the heat, all the comports, usually their collection is $10,000.00 a week, to build a church. The largest Protestant denomination has over 2,000 missionaries in the field that they sponsor, to tell the world christ. When you look at the comparison between the two, when you go to a church on Pohnpei, and the widows are out, and you sit on a hard school, and one day or many days, you can watch an old lady put a penny or two pennies in the collection plate, whereas in America, they can put as much as $100.00 a Sunday, average, at a large church with 1,400 members. But on Pohnpei a woman can put two pennies in the collection plate because that's all she has. By doing that, she reminds you of the story of Christ and the old woman in the Bible. People in the American Churches would send missionaries all over the world, most recently to Africa, to teach them about Jesus, but when it got down to reality, they might even have Reformed Blacks living next door, and might now even speak to them. If those converts came to America, I don't believe they would even be welcomed in a church, much less welcomed into one of their own homes.

FAMILIES

I can go to Pohnpei and I have two families there who have adopted me as their own son. If I'm hungry, they will feed me. If I need clothes, they will give them to me. If I need a place to sleep I have it for as long as I want, no one would turn me away. Could we say the same thing in American in a middle class neighborhood? If you didn't have a place to sleep could you go stay with your friend or your family? No. Would they give you money to help you? No. Would they give you food? No. But they would probably have two cars, three bedroom house, swimming pool, satellite dish, stereo system, central air-heat, but they'd have too much and they wouldn't help you.

Talking about the youth, American youth look at everything should be given to them for instant gratification. They have said many times over the years that they wouldn't work their way through college, and I've asked myself what do they expect? A silver plate for someone to give you a start in life? My students on Pohnpei, if I told one of them that I liked his shirt, or I liked his pants, or I liked his shoes, because I'm older, he would literally take it off and give it to me. In America, most of the youth have had everything given to them and they don't even know how to say thank you. On Pohnpei, my students would give anything to come and live in America for at least a chance to get an education, no matter how hard it is. The family in America, the parents, in my generation, have lived such a high standard, they have bought their children cars, trucks, stereos, tapes, anything money can buy, they have bought, but they have left the raising of children to people who foolishly enough, would work in the church, YMCA, or the Boys' Club to do the raising of their children.

LIAISON OFFICES

Ever since Micronesia came under the Compact of Free Association, the United States is furnishing the government with Liaison Offices. It's like another word for Ambassador Offices. Official there told me that he could not get Americans to come there unless, first of all, the United States would build them tennis courts, a sauna bath, and swimming pools. You have to remember that you are in a third world country and you at least want to be liked by the locals, and when you see kids that can't even buy a coke, just stand and watch these rich Americans, only wishing for an old shirt, I call these people wimps and pansies.

DEMOCRACY

In Micronesia, you have free elections. The United States gives Micronesia a block sum for the government to do with pretty much what it please. What's strange about a democracy is that you get to see it growing from the ground up. They don't have to go through a revolution, for their independence, or a war between the states as we did to preserve our Constitution, and our Democracy. What's weird about their democracy is a Congressman from Micronesia makes thirty thousand dollars a year, a teacher, the highest paid employee on the Island makes only $3,000.00 a year. China is coming around to the leaders in Micronesia, picking them up in airplanes, and carrying them to Peking. They show them how good the Communist form of government is, where everybody is supposed to make the same amount and be treated the same, and to a Micronesian, when he sees that a Congressman makes $30,000.00 a year and a teacher $3,000.00, it looks real good. In Micronesia, the locals are more interested in teaching their kids how to use a machete like an artist does a brush, and trying to live for food the next day, than to try to understand the Super Power struggles, when in

Micronesia time means nothing and food is the most important thing in a person's life. They do not understand political struggles between East and West philosophy, but they're caught in the middle of it and they are hurting.

MY JOB AND NOW IMPORTANT IT IS

I feel that if the American Indian had been able to read, write and speak English that we could very well be an Indian speaking language today in America. They would not have been done so dirty. My job is important as a person, my students will be able to read, write, and speak English. And no one will be able to make a fool of them. That is the importance of my job.

I come back from Micronesia a different person. I know that the most important thing in your life is your health. Without good health, you can do anything, nothing, no matter how much money, you can't buy your health, you can't buy it. You also enjoy such simple things as good water, ice, hot baths, or a nice John to sit on.

No matter how much people will put you down because of jealously, envy, or greed, when you finish up work in Peace Corps you know you don't have to prove anything to anybody and you can do whatever you have the will to do.

The budget for Peace Corps is the lowest of any Federal Agency. The budget is half of what a B-1 bomber cost but what Peace Corps does is it sends people into the poorest of the poor nations to teach English, a trade, health care. As I read once wise words that said, "Give me a fish today and I will be full, teach me how to fish and I will never go hungry." Today all over the world America is hated. Every day on T.V. some nation is burning our flag. It's open season on us. The world is so small and we have to as a free nation understand and look at how people of other nations see the world and how they see us. Peace Corps puts Americans in nations so that they can see and understand us.

As my grandmother used to tell me "Son, the only Jesus most people will ever see is you." That scares me then and now. In Micronesia, the only American most will ever see is me and that also scares me because I'm not worthy. America is known for freedom, rights, the Marshall Plan, rebuilding Japan Germany. After World War the only time in history a victor gave freedom back to the conquered.

LAST SPEECH BEFORE I LEFT—TO MY STUDENTS

I wonder if I've touched a life on Pohnpei. Was my job important here? Your teachers tell me that one day when you are out of school that you will call or write, "Can I come to Alabama to get an education?" OH how you're going to need help in every way. I've lived in both worlds, Pohnpein and American. The plane trip off the Island will be the longest day of your lives. Leaving your close knit family, laid back society where time is not a factor into an airport where you hope to find a friendly face, one to shake your hand and give you a hug and say WELCOME. You're in a big city, you know nobody, no work experience, no car, the most you have may be $50.00. You need a place to live, clothes, what school do you choose, test to be taken, finding a job, a church, everybody speaks English, no one touches you. You're used to being touched, all the cars, horns, everybody is going somewhere so fast. Who is going to be your friend? When you get a car or rent a room, who is going to help you so you don't get cheated. You're going to need a friend, someone to talk to you, someone who cares about you, someone to tell you, "You're loved" and you're not alone. I'm with you as I feel now, I've needed and wanted friends and you were there. Maybe one day, good Lord willing, I can accept you in my home as you have me. God Bless everybody and I love you all.

THE END!

BY:
Frank Burkett

THIS BOOK WAS WRITTEN BY: ALL copy-rights his

EDWARD FRANKLIN BURKETT
418-88-3777
11/24/55
PYONGTAEK UNIVERSTY
111 YONG-YEE-DONG
PYONGTAEK CITY
SOUTH KOREA 450-701

billyjack41@hotmail.com
outsidercastle16@hotmail.com

OR
KWAK, WOO-SOON
JEUNG-SAN-DONG
SAN 10-HAN-sin-Villa
4-dong-ROOM 103
SEOUL 122-936
SOUTH KOREA

011-9364-0832
wings1126@yahoo.co.kr

0-595-32986-1